Praise for *The Rome Zoo*

'Pascal Janovjak evokes a memory of this fantastical place with a concisely efficient pen, but it is also an ingenious and dark-humoured re-writing of the present.' —Lucie Tardin, *Viceversa littérature*

'In a poetic narrative, Pascal Janovjak intertwines the history of the Rome Zoo with a story of impossible love.' —Jean-Claude Perrier, *Livres hebdo*

'Pascal Janovjak captures the melancholic atmosphere of zoos, overlaid here by the tale of a brewing fiasco, with a gently caustic lightness of touch.' —Alain Nicolas, *L'Humanité*

'*The Rome Zoo* is a work of striking originality … the book revisits the history of Italy from 1911 to the present day, interweaving a story of impossible love replete with its own astonishing twists and turns.' —Martine Freneuil, *Le quotidien du médecin*

'Subtly blends fiction with historical fact, holding up a mirror to our own era to reflect our relationship with nature, the animal world and the "other".' —Julien Burri, *Le Temps*

'Pascal Janovjak has written a literary, philosophical, historical and romantic work of utter originality. A profound meditation on Italy's evolution as seen through the lens of the "lost paradise" of the Villa Borghese, an eccentric reflection of our own society.' —Marie-Lucile Kubacki, *La Vie*

‘Straddling historical truth and poetic fiction, Pascal Janovjak populates his novel with a cast of original characters from the past to the present in a beautifully paced narrative. A singular and exhilarating journey.’ —Héloïse Rocca, *Version femina*

‘Interweaving authentic facts with an imagined framework, this tragi-comedy plunges us into the intimist sealed universe of a strange Roman theatre, a mythologised bazaar, still resonating with the muffled echoes of its variously prosperous bygone eras.’ —Michel Bertrou, *La Semaine véterinaire*

‘Pascal Janovjak depicts us to be the products of history we are, revealing our connection to nature as more complex than might at first appear. Ultimately, there is a poetry of sorts in this earthly paradise, this lost ark able to carry us away in the very heart of the city ... *The Rome Zoo* resists easy categorisation.’ —Christophe Henning, *RCF*

‘A magnificent layering of eras.’ —Pierre Maury, *Le Soir*

‘An elegant and refined text, its controlled tone and subtle sense of humour work to displace us temporally, leaving us in a dream-like present on the edges of modernity, where the everyday, rendered with the consistency almost of a mirage, serves as an echo chamber of the past.’ —Riccardo Borghesi, *L’Italie à Paris.net*

Born in Basel in 1975 to a French mother and a Slovakian father, PASCAL JANOVJAK studied comparative literature and art history in Strasbourg before working in the Middle East. His works include *Coléoptères* (*Beetles*), *L'Invisible* (*The Invisible One*) and *À Toi* (*To You*, co-written with Kim Thuy). He now lives in Rome. In 2020 he received the Swiss Literature Award, the Prix Michel-Dentan and the Prix du public de la RTS.

STEPHANIE SMEE left a career in law to work as a literary translator. Recent translations include Hannelore Cayre's *The Inheritors* and *The Godmother* (winner of the CWA Crime Fiction in Translation Dagger award); Françoise Frenkel's rediscovered World War II memoir, *No Place to Lay One's Head*, which was awarded the JQ–Wingate Prize; and Joseph Ponthus's prize-winning work *On the Line*.

THE ROME ZOO

Published by Black Inc.,
an imprint of Schwartz Books Pty Ltd
Level 1, 221 Drummond Street
Carlton VIC 3053, Australia
enquiries@blackincbooks.com
www.blackincbooks.com

Original title: *Le Zoo de Rome*

English translation by Stephanie Smee, 2021
This edition published in 2021

9781760642754 (paperback)
9781743821855 (ebook)

A catalogue record for this
book is available from the
National Library of Australia

Text design and typesetting by Zenobia Ahmed
Cover image by Robert Havell after John James Audubon

Printed in Australia by McPherson's Printing Group.

This project has been assisted by the Australian Government
through the Australia Council, its arts funding and advisory body.

THE ROME ZOO

PASCAL JANOVJAK

Translated by
STEPHANIE SMEE

The man's name is Chahine Gharbi, born 18 April 1970, of Algerian nationality. This is what he wrote in the reception register, five minutes earlier. Here, he'll be known simply as number 324, by reference to the room he'll be occupying from 28 December to 16 January, breakfast included, and this new identity suits him just fine.

There he is, standing in that room, in the grey dawn light. He has not yet removed his coat. He's facing a man who's wearing the hotel's uniform: the man brings his wrists together, like a prisoner's but with thumbs interlaced, and his long fingers unfurl gently as his hands rise up, his fingers fan out and fold back in against the sky of room 324 – two great black wings with pale palms that climb, hover and float back down in the grey dawn.

The Algerian admires the noble wingspan of the hands, but he doesn't seem to grasp the meaning of this charade, nor see the enormous structure that is visible through the umbrella pines outside, and which the bellboy revealed when drawing back the curtains. It must be said that he's tired, that he hasn't asked for any of this. But the bellboy persists, he starts clawing the air, baring predatory teeth and rolling the whites of his eyes – a tiger, or maybe a lion, Chahine thinks, it's hard to say, and now a monkey: the man is swinging his long arms, moving back and forth in room number 324, and while this does have the effect of being even more dramatic, it is also equally and entirely uncalled for. Chahine is relieved when the door closes behind the hotel employee, who has nevertheless done his best. These foreign languages really are such a drag, thinks the bellboy as he returns to his post, which is exactly what Chahine is thinking as he sits down on the bed.

He still hasn't removed his coat. Next to him is a suitcase he is reluctant to open, and a telephone which could do with recharging sooner rather than later. His gaze drifts around the room which feels so familiar, because it's identical to so many others, in other places. A room that's a little larger than it needs to be, just enough to give an impression of luxury. An armchair upholstered in a fabric that's almost certainly red and gold, a picture swallowed up in the half-light, the details of which Chahine struggles to make out.

Outside, the umbrella pines trace their silhouettes against the lines of the great metallic structure. It stands tens of metres tall, the half-sphere, a monument composed of air and steel, of almost equilateral triangles growing ever smaller as they ascend towards its apex. A minor miracle of geometry, even more beautiful now as the first rays of sunshine caress the tubes, causing ridge-lines to glow, giving the half-sphere a new depth. Quietly the dome assumes its position in the surroundings, amongst trees that are gradually colouring up against the deepening blue of the sky. But Chahine is not admiring the spectacle. He has fallen asleep, fully dressed, palms upturned to the ceiling, mouth open. There's no reason to rush. Let's leave him to sleep, he has had a long journey.

As the twentieth century dawns, there is no metal sphere to be seen, no umbrella pines, nor is there any hotel. Just an unmarked area on the edge of the city, wild grasses and a few ill-defined and poorly cultivated plots. A farmer and his ox turn over the fertile soil, under the eye of a small group of dignitaries in patent leather shoes, gathered around a man who is sizing up the area.

Karl Hagenbeck is sporting a large beard in the style of Abraham Lincoln, but white, which underlines his natural authority as an animal tamer and dealer. This is a man who brings in vessels loaded with tigers and cannibals from the most inaccessible of lands, a man who bears the scent of Africa, who behind him has a continent of growling wild beasts, of infinite expanses of savannah and hostile jungle. And Rome is entranced, with only its yellowing statues as reminders of the epic battles between man and beast – marble lions and broken-winged eagles, an entire mythology in the process of crumbling away. Rome, too, wants the sound of roaring as evening falls, wants fangs and knives, the muffled, feverish sound of drums, and the flickering of a campfire on black skin. It's all the more pressing now things are not going so well in Africa, for the Italians. They're annoyed at the sight of their neighbours carving up the world between them, while they themselves are still busy building a country. But first things first. While they wait for the return of their empire, they will at least have a zoo.

Now here's a man who can deliver them Africa on its knees, ankles and wrists bound, along with Asia, the Amazon and both poles. The Jardin Zoologique d'Acclimatation in Paris will pale by comparison with Hagenbeck on board – that's what they told Ernesto Nathan, the mayor, and Ernesto Nathan has no reason to doubt that assessment upon seeing the tall German man smile as he scans the vast construction site, the battalions of labourers now busy digging, packing down, levelling, against a procession of Percheron draught horses hauling loads of earth. Nathan himself is not smiling. He is wondering how much all of this is going to cost him, because he is already busy building law courts, an Olympic stadium and a monument, of ample dimensions, to Vittorio Emanuele which will be visible from a great distance, like the Eiffel Tower. Now all of this is an expensive exercise, he confides to Hagenbeck, and Hagenbeck contents himself with a smile, gracefully stepping over the puddles of water which the other man is forced to skirt. Without pausing too long to consider the financial details, the German sets out his unwavering vision for this zoological garden of the modern age, much like the one he has already built in Hamburg. It is not enough to plant trees and map out promenades. The entire area must be landscaped, the terracing reconstructed, hills fashioned, which will provide the theatre for animal life. Moats, imperceptible to the onlooker, will be excavated, and then Inuits can be positioned in the foreground, Deer behind them and Polar Bears right towards the back – or Nubians, Antelopes and Tigers, as you wish. Most importantly, there'll be no walls, no bars: visitors will be able to take in all these species with a single, admiring glance, it will be a vision of perfect co-existence, an illusion of utmost freedom. Nathan well appreciates the beauty of this vision, even if there has never been any question of exhibiting Inuits here – the only ones, in his view, deserving of a capital letter. No matter, says Hagenbeck, we can install seals in their place, the important thing is to afford a modicum of respect to the notion of climatic coherence. We'll put the amphitheatre over there at the back, two thousand seats, where we'll exhibit the trained animals, and then, over there, the main restaurant where people will be able to have a Wiener schnitzel.

Hagenbeck is smiling because never has he had so much space at his disposal, nor such a budget: while the little mayor of Rome counts his pennies, he, Karl Hagenbeck, is re-creating Paradise on Earth.

When he leaves the hotel, Chahine is a little more alert: on waking up, he even thought to slip his magnetic key card into the box next to the door, thereby illuminating the whole room, and the screen of his telephone. Now he has everything he needs, a phone that is more or less recharged, a black briefcase that makes him look professional, a clean shirt and a freshly shaven chin. He is also very late: it's already 1.00 pm, they're waiting for him in a restaurant, the address of which he enters into his phone as he goes down the front steps.

Chahine doesn't have to think about anything else, he just has to do his best to keep the little blue dot that represents him moving forward for as long as it takes to complete the map's precisely calculated journey: go left, then take the first street on the left and continue straight on to the red pin. Child's play really, a route of seven hundred and forty metres, but one during which Chahine narrowly avoids bumping into a poorly parked car, then a dog, then the dog's master, because he's walking with eyes glued to the screen and to the hesitant progress of the little blue dot which is turning left at the same time its flesh-and-blood double is heading up a raised pathway, lined with railings. On the screen, this path crosses a large grey featureless expanse, because the zoo does not constitute public open space – but Chahine is not aware of this.

Is he also unaware of the smells brought out by the humidity? The strange cries emerging from the vegetation, the calls that tickle his eardrums? Who knows. For animals, every significant perception results in a physical reaction even if it is, itself, insignificant; it's more complicated with humans, their subconscious occasionally interferes – not to mention the fact that humans love nothing more than to pretend not to notice things. Perhaps that's what Chahine is doing now, with some considerable effort: he's focusing on his screen, certainly doesn't notice the monumental aviary rising up on his left, doesn't see the fake rocks appearing on either side of the path, or the administrative building, the old entrance to the Reptilarium, the balloon-seller or the balloons in which he now entangles himself, getting caught up in their strings, struggling in vain to extract himself from their ridiculous snares, stifling a curse.

Chahine resigns himself. He's standing at the zoo's monumental entrance. It's difficult to pretend otherwise. It's even engraved in capital letters on either side of the gate:

GIARDINO ZOOLOGICO

– and a furious elephant, mounted above one of the arches, looks down on him, along with a roaring lion, crouching on top of the wall.

The forecourt is deserted this early in the week, and time has stopped. No wind in the acanthus leaves on the columns. The lion roaring on its pedestal no longer moves, the elephant's trunk is fixed in stone, the allegories atop the building have frozen, and Chahine too: he is perfectly immobile, a statue. Only the little balloon-seller bustles about, doing his best to untangle the strings as he circles the careless man and his briefcase. By the time he's finished, the clouds will again be slipping across the December grey, life will have reasserted itself, and a little blue dot on the screen of the telephone will enter, hovering, into uncharted territory.

The majestic neo-Baroque entrance to the zoo is not the work of Karl Hagenbeck, who sighs when he sees the model submitted by a certain Brasini: he would have preferred something more Jugendstil in design, something similar to Hamburg, and his team of architects and landscape designers, German and intransigent, are of the same view. But with them is a man who quietly admires the roaring lions, and the Italian savoir faire. There's something unsettling about the fellow, always standing at the back of photographs taken at the time; he wears a big black hat, has a prophet's beard and a gaze that pierces the lens if it isn't wandering out of frame. It so happens that he's Swiss, and an animal sculptor too, he could have been entrusted with the statuary on the entrance gate. But he is not sufficiently talented, probably because he is too fond of his subject matter. They say he breeds hyenas. That he eats the meat, bones and all. That he roars, at dusk. They mutter, looking at his nails, that he paces the streets of Zurich by night in the company of a lioness. It is all entirely true, but it should be noted that the lioness is leashed – and that if he only walks it at night, it's because the Zurich police have requested he no longer do so by day.

It is not for his love of big cats that Hagenbeck has had him come, nor for his skills as a sculptor. Urs Eggenschwyler is an expert in *Zementrabitz,* timber framework dressed in metallic mesh and covered in cement: it is now possible to construct grottos, pyramids or cliffs at relatively little expense. Eggenschwyler has already created the polar landscape at the Hamburg Tierpark, and Hagenbeck is relying on him. For it is the fake rocks, more than the animals, more so than the plants, which make a zoo. Escarpments that suddenly appear out of the ground, mysterious crevices, entire icebergs which seem to have slipped right into the otherwise unremarkable plains of a city: it is this, too, which people come to see, though they may not realise it.

Urs Eggenschwyler travels less, however, than his icebergs, and he is so excited to find himself in Rome that he is not sleeping, or at least is sleeping very poorly. The day after his arrival he dreamed of his friend, the artist Arnold Böcklin, dead ten years earlier. Dressed in a long white shirt, Böcklin came into Urs' bedroom, sat himself down at his bedside and, without moving his lips, ordered him to build a full-scale reproduction of his most famous painting, *Isle of the Dead*, in the zoo's central lake.

As Urs recounts his dream, with trembling voice and eyes ablaze, Hagenbeck gives him his full attention. He nods his head, puts a hand on Urs' shoulder. He understands the significance of this vision, of Böcklin's wish. Yes, of course, the isle of the dead, right there, in the middle of the lake, with its peaks and its caverns and its cypress pines – he brings his face close to the haggard features of his friend, his sideburns merging with the other's bushy beard – between you and me, yes, I quite understand how it might seem imperative, to recreate the landscape of that mythical painting here, right here. But the Romans ... I already know what they're going to say.

They'll tell me their city has more than enough tombs to be going on with. They're not like us, Hagenbeck adds under his breath, *sie können die Geister nicht hören*, we are the only ones able to understand such things. But fear not, says the German, delicately detaching his whiskers from the Swiss man's beard, we shall see, let me speak to them, I'll take care of it. Urs leaves, eyes shining, heart pounding, while Hagenbeck regrets having put his collaborators up in the same hotel as himself.

As he has done every morning since his arrival, he hunches over the sketches strewn across the desk in his hotel suite. He starts by running his finger over the future restaurant, at the elevated north end of the site. A large restaurant, a generous terrace overlooking the gardens. Then, as he has done every morning, Hagenbeck sits down on a wrought-iron chair which does not yet exist, his back to the building which does not yet exist, facing his dream. He starts by placing his right elbow on the back of the chair, as if turning to the west: there in the distance, the tip of the iceberg is shining in the morning light, a brighter splotch sparkles in its crevices, a white bear, above the sea lions' pool – closer to him, five kangaroos hop about along the shores of the lake where pink flamingos, red ibises and a few sultan chickens plump and ruffle their feathers. Hagenbeck stretches his legs now and looks straight ahead: the sun plays on the still water, a pair of mandarin ducks takes flight, passes over the lake, flies over a group of gazelles and some zebras grazing in their field, under the watchful gaze of the big cats dozing in their shadowy caves in the midday heat. If you're lucky, you might even see the peculiar horns of the Nigerian giraffe slip between the lions' crag and the tigers' rock. It's magnificent, Hagenbeck tells himself, a postcard landscape. And there's Eggenschwyler, who would ruin all that with his isle of the dead, who would block out the entire view. He'll have to make sure the man doesn't mention it to anybody, you just never know, the Romans are quite capable of agreeing to it. They've already insisted on building a neo-Baroque entrance gate, which just goes to show – and Hagenbeck, shifting a little to the left and towards the east, spies it behind the ostrich enclosure, next to the elephant house. It has been days now that he has been telling himself that something is needed there, something to hide it entirely, that entrance gate. A little something should be built so the goats and chamois can gambol about over there, as the sun goes down. It would be pretty. It would provide a counterpoint to the iceberg, and would keep Urs occupied too.

She had raised the collar of her coat, it had started to rain and the occasional drops pattered on the green water of the seals' basin. There was only one, as it happened, turning circles, its oily rocket-shaped body brushing past the cement edges – it lifted its head for a moment to yawn, surprising her with the astonishing red of its maw against the dirty grey of its body, a set of pointed teeth standing out against the bright, gleaming red; she hadn't thought seals would have such sharp teeth. But it closed its jaws and resumed its monotonous round, and Giovanna continued with her visit. She followed the gentle slope down to the little lake and to the Oasis Bar, where nobody served her a coffee, despite the counter in the hut being illuminated. A few ducks were paddling at the lake's edge, and over everything could be heard the pump gurgling as it tried to recycle water thick with dust. Beyond the picnic tables, two swings, condemned by plastic tape, were creaking in the wind. A wooden bridge led to the other side of the lake towards a path strewn with dead leaves. The daunting vegetation muffled the noise of the city, creating a brooding, thick silence shot through with the sound of cries and rustling. She felt increasingly oppressed by her solitude; from time to time she caught a glimpse of a keeper's face, behind a barrier, and she had the disagreeable sensation that somebody was spying on her. The zoo's director had, however, suggested he accompany her, she had declined, but she realised now that to have come incognito did not mean she would go unnoticed. The ash blonde of her hair perhaps had something to do with it, her slender figure – that said, her femininity had no effect on the creatures: the only animal gaze she encountered was the oblique, uneasy look of a peacock as it crossed the path and a camel who watched her, chewing its cud, from its shelter. In fact, perhaps it was a dromedary, only its head was visible, in any event Giovanna had never been able to remember the hump rule, she would hardly have been surprised to see it had three. She then encountered a *Tamandino africano* and a *Casuario elmato* depicted on information panels telling her that the first was a sort of anteater and the second an ostrich from New Guinea, both species under threat of extinction which would have been interesting to observe, had these specimens not preferred to remain invisible. Giovanna then looked for the bear enclosure and its much-vaunted refurbishment, and then finding herself trapped on unused paths cut off by barriers covered in yellowing signs, she found herself simply trying to work out where she was. The visitors' map was truly hopeless, or had somebody remodelled the zoo overnight? She ought to have been in front of the Tigers' Rock now, and not at the foot of the steps leading to the Great Aviary. It must be said, Giovanna did not have much of a sense of direction. It is possible she was also a little anxious; it wasn't the first time she had visited the zoo, but from now on she was responsible for it. The announcement had not yet been made, but Giovanna Di Stefano had just been appointed *General Manager and Head of Marketing and Communications* – and this double-barrelled title said as much about the state of its finances as did the broken steps she was now ascending.

Every one of her observations amounted to the beginnings of a file which would need to be dealt with, whether it concerned infrastructure upkeep or management of sales outlets. But even more disconcerting was the inertia of the place. Its lack of highlights or drawcards. How could she sell the spectacle of that stork standing there, immobile, amidst a constellation of bird droppings, of that ibis asleep on its branch? None of these animals appeared to her to be any more alive than in a documentary on a plasma screen. Did people even watch animal documentaries anymore, Giovanna wondered, as she considered the balding, limping marabou. A voice crackled over the loudspeakers, announcing closing time, and the message drifted, echoing, along the deserted paths. The institution was heading for disaster. The private companies sitting on the board were refusing to invest another cent and appeared indifferent to the imminent catastrophe. It was a vicious circle: no public, insufficient revenue to cater for them appropriately. There was no point deluding oneself; she would start with the little things, make a list of urgent matters, check the basics, answer the most pressing needs, thought Giovanna, following the sign pointing to the nearest restrooms.

The toilets were not as dirty as she was expecting, but were still too dusty for her liking. There was no toilet paper, every corner had its spiderwebs, and there was no mirror. The men's room couldn't be in any better state: but to satisfy herself, she took a deep breath and pushed open the adjacent door, only to find herself face to face with a fellow leaning against the wall next to the basins. I just need to charge my phone, mumbled the foreigner, the first thing he said, as if he were the intruder, and she, caught by surprise herself, started stammering foolishly as she closed the door again, perhaps also because the man had very dark eyes, or perhaps because he had spoken in French. But scarcely had she taken two steps when she recovered her composure, reminded herself of her position and, probably prompted also by a hint of curiosity, did an about-face in order to let the man know that the zoo was about to close. He'd not had time to move or to wipe away his sheepish smile. He nodded and she noticed then the incongruous cord emerging from his trouser pocket, attaching him to the power point in the wall. Giovanna pursed her lips at the sight of this man recharging himself. On reflection, perhaps this job would be more entertaining than she was expecting – this time, when she closed the door, it was to hide an irrepressible smile.

Hagenbeck's sketches are passed around. They're fleshed out by the architects: the elephant house will be a sober, pharaoh-esque Art Nouveau affair, they'll build a mosque to scale with the giraffes, with carved mashrabiya lattice-work and a dome, and for the ostriches, a small Moorish fort, with a Byzantine cupola atop alternating black and white stonework. The entire behind-the-scenes aspect also needs to be designed: the fake rocks are hollow, with service corridors, storage areas, cages slotted into them. Plans go backwards and forwards between design studios and hotel rooms, the landscape designer plants a few trees, conifers near the Nordic settings and palms everywhere else, shrubs, bushes and ferns to hide the infrastructure, so these other-worldly temples will blend into an ancient scenery of plant life. And corrections are scribbled, embellishments added, behind the big cats' rocks there'll be bas-reliefs initially imagined as Sumerian, then Inca, before opting for something subtly Babylonian-Aztec. On paper everything is progressing well enough, but things become complicated when the drawings are to be transferred onsite and become solid structures. Things aren't always clear, there are walls heading off in the wrong direction, moats cutting across pathways, the orangutan pavilion rises askew, the reptile house is punctured by windows which shouldn't be there. The Italians start doubting the Germans' common sense, the Germans start doubting the interpreters, there's arguing, hats are dashed to the ground, contradictory plans are brandished – and then eventually they are turned back up the right way and everything works out, or almost everything. The finishing touches are applied. Centuries of erosion are drawn onto rocks that are not yet dry, some Somalian huts are added for the American bison, an Indian setting for the cervids, there's no longer any time for splitting hairs. There's still a small corner, over there, for the brown bears and the wolf packs, it's a bit tight, it'll do.

No fewer than five Italian engineers have come, Ernesto Nathan has been waiting for them in what's to be the administration building, he listens to their heavy, anxious steps on the stairs – when they come in they look carefully right and left, making sure they're alone, and then they start: nothing is on track anymore, *signor sindaco*, it's a disaster, too many delays, they're all speaking at the same time, they're gesturing with their hands, fingers steepled, they raise their arms heavenwards, they point to the floor. In the end, Nathan is made to understand that the lighting needs to be rethought, which he knew, but also that the sewer system needs to be revisited, which he did not. Hagenbeck has priorities, everything at eye-level, landscaping and animals, everything either above or below has been neglected. Now there really isn't a lira left to be had, they have insufficient cement, they have insufficient everything, especially time: *un disastro, signor sindaco.*

The mayor of Rome clasps his hands behind his back. He takes two steps across the parquetry floor which is still covered in sawdust, but is already creaking. He knows they're right. He turns his back to them and moves over to the window, he looks out to the Matterhorn which is backlit against the sun. It's impressive, the Matterhorn in Rome. It's where Hagenbeck has chosen to have the ibex frolicking. And it has some appeal, the outline of scaffolding against the shapeless mass of the mountain, with its saw-tooth relief. A figure is moving about up there. He recognises the man by his abundant beard: it's the Swiss sculptor, Eggenschwyler, who is skilfully slashing into the cement, in a frenzy of high spirits. He, for one, looks happy.

Nathan unfolds his hands. Behind him, the five engineers still have their fingertips pressed together, they're waiting. Then the mayor of Rome turns to them and speaks. It's just a rough version of the speech he will give on 20 June 1910 at the Teatro Argentina to the audience of backers of the public company, but it is already very convincing: where there's a will there's a way, basically. With the result that it's five men, brave of heart, who head back down the stairs, their step a little lighter now, taking with them every ounce of his remaining energy. Nathan turns back to the Matterhorn, he's thinking back to the stories he heard as a child, of Babylon and the ziggurat, fables he sweeps away with an impatient hand.

Almost a century later, a little bald man was standing at that same window, at the same time of day. The outlook may well have changed but he was not interested in the outlook, or in what the zoo's director was telling him from his seat in the big leather armchair behind him. He had stopped listening a long time ago, he had even been forced to turn his back on him just to tolerate his presence. Guido Anselmo Moro was more interested in this woman walking back up the path. He was observing her closely, over the top of his little round spectacles: she had just emerged from the underground passage, her gait was smooth and determined, a little too hurried – she stopped reluctantly at the pygmy hippopotamus pool, a keeper had just called out to her. What bad luck! The only chatty keeper in the place, sixty-three years old, forty of them spent within the confines of the zoo: he always had a tale to tell, never missed an opportunity, especially if it involved a pretty woman. From up at his window, Moro admired the keeper's tactics; he was going to leave his hose to approach his victim, never taking his eyes off her, so he could ensnare her in some endless saga. Moro loved observing any creature: he held a doctorate in ethology and was also the zoo's chief scientist. He knew all its inhabitants and every one of its staff, and he also knew who the ash-blonde woman was. It was how she now reacted which interested him. He saw her white hand come out of her coat pocket to signal some other objective, an excuse, but he also noticed the hesitation, her chest struggling to follow the direction of the movement. No doubt she feared rubbing the old keeper up the wrong way; she would be his superior. But on that point she was already mistaken: it was he, Doctor Moro, who was responsible for the keepers, for recruiting them and for their well-being, just as he was for the animals. But that she would learn soon enough. What bothered him more was her hesitation. Moro doesn't like people who hesitate. It's dangerous. Take the keepers, for example: they hesitate just a fraction, in a cage, and they'll lose a hand. Animals don't hesitate. They are wary. It's a very different thing.

The woman had just turned her head: another figure had appeared on the path, grey coat and briefcase, short hair olive skin about forty. Not somebody Moro recognised, just a visitor, but he took note of his step, a little too short for his height, and one shoulder lower than the other, as if the small briefcase were weighing him down. The man straightened up, however, on noticing the woman and the keeper, he walked past behind her – and for a moment she made as if to fix her hair, so she could follow him with her eyes. The games we play, thought Moro. Humans might well have built the pyramids and split the atom, but how desperately predictable they still were; none more so than the director speaking behind him, a well-meaning fellow, social and fleshy, an expert in banalities and Calabrian wines. To begin with, Moro had observed him as he would a rare specimen, fascinated by the profound stupidity of a man who nonetheless had acquired responsibilities – and then he had discerned in him that blend of opportunism and mental laziness affecting so many of his kind, at which point he had stopped listening to him. It had its advantages, a superior fool: Moro had only to put forward an idea for the director to repeat it to anyone who would listen, which explained, moreover, why he was still there despite his track record of poor figures.

Outside, they were closing the gates behind the sole visitor of the afternoon, as the woman with the ash-blonde hair finally put an end to the keeper's chatter: her shoulders already turning away, she listened to one last comment, shifted a foot forwards, nodded again and ended up extracting herself from his clutches to resume her route towards the administration building, accelerating as she walked, now it had even become a little race, she was approaching and you could hear the clicking of her heels on the bitumen and on the front steps, below, exactly two floors beneath Moro who removed his spectacles and rubbed his nose.

'You'll forgive me, won't you? I'm sorry, I wasn't listening. You were saying?'

'That she should be here any moment now. You'll see, I've heard only good things about her, she really is just the person we need.'

Moro smiled. The director didn't need anything, it was he, Moro, who had needs, and plans.

'See, what was I just saying, I can hear her on the stairs . . .'

Yes, thought Moro, but she was going to stop by the bathroom first. Relieve her pressing need and then look at herself in the mirror. Perhaps take the time to redo her make-up, if she was wearing any. Finally, he was going to be able to observe her from up close.

The animals arrive in the capital in the middle of the night, on the 2nd of November 1910. They number a thousand or so. The usual smell of a goods station, soot and grease, is suddenly charged with the heavier stench of other odours, firstly the smell of straw and excrement and the slurry that is pouring out from the open goods carriages, sweeping ahead of it the smallest of the cadavers. Numerous animals have not survived the journey, various of them were already unwell on leaving Hamburg, the carriage floors are strewn with bodies, nobody knows which bodies or how many, they'll have to wait for dawn to do a detailed inventory. For all Hagenbeck's experience in the transportation of wild animals, he expected losses in the order of at least twenty per cent each move. That was an average. In any event, everything will have been replaced in a month or two, the most important thing is that the big animals have made it, the ones with the trunks and the long necks – the truth of it is that visitors rarely come to admire a lemur. That night there are dozens of curious onlookers, and those who are not horrified by the smell or put off by the late hour experience the delight of seeing crates, cages and cinched-up pachyderms swinging through the skies above them at the station in the beams of acetylene lamps, hoisted by small cranes into wagons, and in the confusion of off-loading, rubberneckers are keen to fight their way through, to get a better view, inspect the bottom of cages, make out the breathing. All that can be heard is the sound of slamming doors, the puttering of motors and men shouting, men giving orders and waving their arms about in the crazed flashing of lantern beams.

They had two months to settle the animals, to distribute them into their settings, to check the locks on the cages and go over the restaurant menu. Astonishingly enough, the deadlines were met. A quick sweep of the paths. On the 5th of January 1911, Rome's Zoological Gardens were opened. It was the first event held to celebrate the fiftieth anniversary of Italy's Unification.

Chahine looks at himself in the photo booth. He'll soon be forty, as will the face on the screen. Yet he's struggling to recognise himself. Truth be told, he feels as though his hair should be a little longer, his skin not quite so pale. The absence of shadows under his eyes surprises him too, notwithstanding the weight of the fatigue he feels has settled there. Right at that moment, alone with nothing but this face in front of him, he could probably still change the course of events. Return to Algiers. His business partner was irritated, Chahine had claimed a plane delay, an issue with the taxi, he was feeling faint, and the meeting had been pushed back. Yes, perhaps it would be better to return. But not today, today nothing would distract him from his objective. There was certainly no shortage of diversions, he could visit Saint Peter's Basilica, or the Piazza Navona, or the Church of Saint Charles at the Four Fountains, or go to swoon before Bernini's *Ecstasy of Saint Teresa* – all things on which the receptionist's zealous pen had landed, insisting on writing down distances and bus routes, covering the paper with such a tangle of lines that Chahine could not have followed them, even had he wanted to. The foreigner had been happy to listen to the fulsome instructions, before asking once again, this time perhaps articulating a little more clearly, where one could take photos – no, not photos of the city, photos of himself, a machine that would take photos of him.

All the same, there is little room for doubt; the face on the photo booth screen is his. When he stretches his mouth to one side, the face on the screen does the same, and when he closes an eye too – but if he closes his right eye, the other face closes the opposite one, the left one. So it's an anti-Chahine being displayed back to him by the machine, an inverse Chahine. Or, more simply put, a reflection. But for Chahine nothing at the moment is really simple and even the countdown catches him unawares, perhaps because the numbers are reeled off in Italian, or because he's wondering if the shot will be taken on 'zero' or right afterwards – regardless, the flash takes him by surprise, as does the sight of the ankle boots that appear under the curtain. Just the boots of somebody waiting their turn, but it's annoying, to be bothered like that in such intimate circumstances. They ought to have had a curtain that fell lower, Chahine thought, hesitating to draw it back: 35, 40 centimetres, that's all you'd need. Of course, if you were to do it, you'd have to allow, say, closer to 30 centimetres, so the bottom of the curtain didn't get dirty, he thinks, looking at the ankle boots that are now inside the booth, it being not entirely clear how that bodily exchange took place.

In the bus, Chahine inspects the four shots, one by one. They are completely identical, and he recognises himself in none of them. They dropped into the photo booth slot like any can of fizzy drink, but without making the slightest noise. It weighs nothing, a man's face.

From its first year of life, the superb Rome Zoo has been struggling. When it opened, people beat a path to its gate, and then, well, they had seen it. The general public are like sheep, and there's nothing more distressing for Romans than finding themselves in a place where they don't know anybody; their whole reputation is undermined.

The wind is blowing across the deserted restaurant terrace, and not a soul is there to enjoy the view across to Paradise. It really is a pity, particularly given the considerable cost involved in the upkeep of Hagenbeck's landscaping. The lions are suffering from their northern exposure, while the polar bears struggle to find any shade. Under the hyenas' watchful gaze the zebras are trembling, refusing to eat, and the antelopes are terrified too, stumbling and falling into the moats. They're just details but adjustments need to be made, ideas revisited. Sacrifice the clarity of the setting to ward off the sun's intensity, plant some plane trees and acacias. And so the perfect landscape is already changing, subjected to the dictates of the teeming life it shelters, and the vagaries of the climate. It took only a breath of wind to bring the Matterhorn down: a timber frame erected in haste, a minor defect in the cement . . . It had trembled a little, then collapsed, generating a huge amount of dust; nobody was there to witness the formidable spectacle, the terrified bleating of the izards caught in the rubble. It won't be rebuilt, there is just enough money to clear it away.

It cost 1,477,147 liras to build the zoo, and there's really nothing to know about exchange rates in the year 1911 that would render that sum any less intimidating, an amount, moreover, which exceeded budget predictions by a good third. There would appear to have been forecasting errors. With an entrance fee of half a lira, it's suddenly apparent that it has not been paid off, and is unlikely to be while the city numbers only 542,123 inhabitants – not all of whom are wildlife enthusiasts. It's small, the city of Rome, in 1911, an oversized village on the banks of the Tiber, and while these days the zoo might look like a blemish buried in the capital, at the time it constituted a second city, a city of animals located an endless commute from the centre. For want of any better idea a tramline is built, a brand spanking new tram that rattles along from the centre of town to the northern outskirts, where it sets you down like a flower at the gates. It's not enough to bring in the crowds but it's quite practical nonetheless – it's the same tram jolting and clattering along that Giovanna uses to get to her office where she greets some staff whose names she still doesn't know, and opens account ledgers which, a century later, are no closer to adding up.

Giovanna's office is dilapidated and damp, much less comfortable than the one she used to have at the municipal council. She had contributed to Veltroni's win, and three years later Alemanno's team had pushed her towards the exit: having enjoyed a position at the helm of the city, Giovanna now found herself in charge of its zoo. It was a position that would cast a minor shadow over her career, but Giovanna hated nothing more than inactivity. Admittedly, the product she was required to promote was a little unusual. She could sense its vaguely oppressive presence, all that mute life stirring around her, the fruity aroma wafting into her office, through the windows that didn't close properly. She'd had a nightmare about it the previous evening, imagining things scratching at her bedroom window, the beating of black wings. Her husband had reassured her, stroking her shoulder, but in her dream his hand had turned into a spider, and she had screamed.

Her predecessor had resigned in a rush of blood, they said he had gone abroad to take the waters. He had left nothing for Giovanna, nothing but a cupboard full of files, a mountain of outstanding matters and, most importantly, a pile of unpaid invoices. Municipal subsidies were running six months in arrears and they had to prioritise, pay those suppliers who were indispensable and make the others wait, even if those businesses did belong to the director's cousin or to the caretaker's brother-in-law. Pay the important ones first and the urgent ones next, even if Giovanna was not sure she could tell the difference, when it came to such disparate files. One of the restaurants had been accused of food poisoning. Rats had damaged the electrical wiring of the mangabey pavilion, the lemurs' pool pump had just given out, the London Zoo was putting in a claim for an anteater that hadn't arrived – Giovanna had asked her secretary not to put through any calls but that had not protected her from the secretary herself, who was agitating loudly for a new computer, although it was really the entire IT system that needed replacing. Dealing with urgent matters was preventing her from gaining any overview of the whole situation. She had to start with some basic organising, and that morning, in her office, Giovanna set about doing exactly that – a simple, calming task, just to get things underway. It was when she emptied the first drawer that she discovered, to her surprise, a drawing, underneath a pile of loose papers and chewed pens. A poorly executed drawing carved into the wood, depicting a faceless figure, hanging from a set of gallows, alongside the letters *MORO*.

Giovanna wondered if her predecessor really could have been responsible for this sinister but infantile graffiti. It was not impossible. There was no question the chief scientist was capable of having a devastating effect on a fragile personality. Moro had come to see her the previous evening, they had discussed various urgent matters and then he had thrown an amused glance at a bundle of files she had just exhumed which contained details of the zoo's promotional activities. In an apologetic tone, he had enumerated the contents of the folders as if he could see straight through their covers. The red file contained the Christmas program: activities set around the pachyderms, fundraising for farming communities in Sri Lanka, the sale of recycled paper made from elephant dung. They had been rehashing the same activities for four years now, he knew them off by heart, that blue one underneath had the Easter activities: a workshop on oviparous animals, children would be able to touch some ostrich eggs. You should start by tossing it all in the bin, he'd finished, smugly.

Giovanna had gripped her pen more tightly. Why did this little zoologist think he could give her advice? Of course, they would have to come up with some new ideas. But those activities weren't expensive, and first they needed to clean up the budget. The amount allocated to research was excessive, given its minimal impact on the zoo's visibility. While she had set out the areas which would be their future battlegrounds, Moro had scrutinised her face over the top of his small round spectacles. There was no trace of hostility on his part, just manifest curiosity, as if he were looking to grasp something behind words which were not really being directed at him. So she had raised the stakes, announcing redundancies she had identified in the scientific research department, which employed more than half the staff. An urgent need for a redesign of the organisational structure, cuts to payroll, a refocusing of efforts on infrastructure that was going to the dogs. Moro had listened carefully, fingers crossed on his knees, and Giovanna had suddenly felt like a student in an oral exam – an oral exam, moreover, for which she had prepared very poorly. The little man had looked at his watch, as if signalling the end of the exam, then he had stood up, smiling: Yes, we'll have to speak about it again, of course, but I'm not sure you're on the right track with your approach … I believe your pen is leaking, you have ink on your fingers.

And then, just as he was about to leave the room, he had turned back, still smiling: I forgot to tell you. This will make you happy. Last night a little khulan was born. You should go and see it … His smile had broadened, and he had closed the door. She remembered perfectly how his voice had grown suddenly unctuous: … a little khulan was born, Moro had said, saying 'little khulan' the way a child says 'little baby', to emphasise the oh-so-cute nature of the thing. He had been mocking her. Of course, it was significant, the birth of an animal, it was an event that could be sold to hordes of kids and their parents. But not to her, not like that. She pushed the drawer with the gallows closed a little more abruptly than necessary. In any event, she had much more important things to be doing, what did he think, and anyway, what even was a khulan, and where would she find it, Giovanna wondered as she called her secretary.

Nobody knows how Eggenschwyler caught wind of his Matterhorn's collapse, particularly as he was locked up, in Zurich, having once again been found naked in his lioness's enclosure. But from the depths of his cell, using a sheet of paper and what remained of his lucidity, the sculptor wrote to Karl Hagenbeck: It was to be expected, we had been warned by Böcklin's spirit. You refused to build the isle of the dead on the zoo's lake, now your entire Eden is going to drown in it. I tell you, everything in Italy is about to go from bad to worse.

Hagenbeck tosses the letter into the waste paper bin and writes another to Rome's new mayor: Your zoo is too small, it should be expanded, something your predecessor never wanted to do – he was a bit tight with the purse strings, just between you and me. I can source you some Kalmuks, for example, those little Mongolians with the bowed legs, quite entertaining to look at. They put up their tents, cook their food, sing and dance, in Berlin we had 93,000 visitors in one day. Or how about some Indians from Ceylon? Flute players, masked dancers, snake charmers, mahouts and elephants? Some of them are dwarves, in Paris we had a million visitors in two months. They have to be paid, of course, but usually the general public takes care of that by tossing them coins – and they're perfectly inoffensive, you can touch them.

He sets down his pen. He'll let the Romans do their calculations. Let them work out that in the end the Mongolians are a considerably more profitable option: 93,000 tickets, that's the same as two Colosseums packed to the rafters. The fact is that this little tribe of Mongolians are already in Hagenbeck's rear courtyard, and he doesn't know what to do with them. The women have started prostituting themselves, the men are loafing about under their tents, many are sick, stricken by colds which is all it takes to kill them. The children are squabbling in the dirt, Hagenbeck can't bear their screaming anymore, the sound floats up to his office windows. He'd send them happily to hell or at least to Rome, seeing as everybody else in Europe has already seen them.

But the company's shareholders are feeling a little unadventurous. Ten years ago such ethnological spectacles did well, and people remember the Sudanese Dinkas in Milan and the Eritrean villages in Turin. But people also remember the maladies, the unnatural relations, the scandalous love affairs between well-bred young women and men who were quite Somalian, no question about it. At the Vatican, every now and again missionaries bring back some pleasant Indians who've learned to sing clutching a Bible which, you understand, is altogether more decent. And so, they're about to file away the generous offer without any follow up, but look, there's another page; just on the off chance, Hagenbeck attaches a long list of animals to his letter, setting out their rate in German gold marks, taking care to emphasise that the specimens are of excellent quality and that they're being offered at absolutely discounted rates given the long, collaborative relationship he has enjoyed with the Eternal City, and so on and so forth. The company trusts him. They buy some new animals, and on 21 July 1915 the zoo is declared bankrupt.

Behind the ticket-booth glass, three-quarters of Giovanna's face is illuminated, her head tilted down – exactly like Chahine Gharbi's face in the photo lying on the counter, and which she's glancing at out of the corner of her eye.

She had stopped by to enquire about December's poor figures, and also to see where they were with the Family and Friends subscriptions, an unfortunate initiative of her predecessor, advertisements for which had been posted here and there all over the place – only to have the ticket attendant, hiding away her nail polish, announce proudly that she had just sold one, a Family and Friends subscription, just now, isn't that funny? To some guy who has already come five times this week, so you see I offered him a subscription, a Family and Friends subscription because Maurizio, I mean, Signor Catuogno, your predecessor, told us always to begin by offering a Family and Friends subscription so that's what he took, this fellow. In fact, I'm not sure he understood all the advantages of the offer, he doesn't speak Italian and he's always on his own, I noticed him right away because I saw him get tangled up in the balloon-seller's strings last Sunday, the balloon-seller over on the other side of the gate, he was walking along like this, with his eyes down, and he walked straight into all the balloons, you should have seen him, and he's not bad looking, I mean, just between you and me, he looks a bit like that football player, the one who ... Good, says Giovanna, running her eyes over the registration form where the ink is still fresh, yes, would you please remove those kitten pictures behind you, and put up something more serious, maybe a print? And I quite like the designs on your nails but there are other places to do that, and also, you could make a bit more of an effort, I mean, what sort of handwriting is that ... you know, nobody is irreplaceable, and these forms have to be able to be read by other people, what *is* that you've written there?

The name and date of birth which the ticket attendant now reads out in a small voice are, apart from a few mistakes, identical to those noted in the hotel register, at the start of this story. But this form also notes the profession of the subscriber, which Giovanna points out should be written with two 't's, yes, yes, I can assure you, it's written with two 't's, *architetto*, repeats Giovanna to the ticket attendant – who, while looking in the drawer for the correction fluid, blushingly reveals a formidable arsenal of manicure products. And he had no other photo? asks Giovanna, annoyed. Oh yes, I did ask him, says the ticket attendant, and he showed me three others, but they were all the same.

The zoo is placed under the administrative supervision of the municipal council of Rome, and as Eggenschwyler foretold, everything is now going from bad to worse in Italy. Costs continue to soar, because while nobody is going to the restaurant, the animals at the zoo have not stopped eating. This means every year they have to allow for:

- 37,000 kilograms of beef
- 7500 kilograms of potatoes
- 16,700 kilograms of corn
- 4500 eggs
- 13,000 litres of milk

to mention only some of the ingredients required to feed them. That's a lot of milk, 13,000 litres, especially in times of war – for scarcely has the country finished up with the Ottomans in Libya than they're launched into another conflict, this time on a global scale. And while the humans in Rome frantically leaf through the newspapers to find out what their troops are up to in the Alps, the animals carry on living and dying.

The first director, who had accompanied Hagenbeck, is sacked, a certain *Herr Doktor* Knott-Meyer, whose name, in 1915, really does sound a little too Teutonic. And the pen-pushers at the council don't understand a thing about the creatures for whom they're now supposedly responsible. They make cuts, and then are astonished to see crocodiles floating, belly up, in the pool's freezing water. They cut back on rations, and then, dumbstruck, witness the death of the zoo's first Ethiopian: it's spectacular to see a giraffe die. A bit like felling a tree. The gnus and impalas waste away on the yellowing grass of their field, which still hasn't been joined up to the watering system: the keepers go backwards and forwards carrying buckets.

While some animals are disappearing, others just arrive unannounced, like the pink weevils which devour the palm trees, and smaller animals too, that you can't even see. People wonder if it's normal for chamois to have such swollen eyes, all red and weeping. They wonder the same thing when they see the orangutans' backsides.

It's a shame about the irreplaceable losses, the great black rhinoceros which the chief zookeeper was so fond of straddling, a snow leopard that didn't last two days. There are not yet antibiotics, nor is there even a qualified veterinarian – and the keepers spend their time watching animals die, and replacing them. They also receive gifts which they don't always know what to do with, settling them in wherever they can. Sometimes they're lucky, the young Asian cheetah gets along well with the female chimpanzee – but at other times they just can't understand what has happened: no sooner have they pushed the baby Marsican brown bear into its cage than it is ripped to pieces by the two adults already in there. They discover meticulously hollowed-out tortoise shells, in the porcupine enclosure. They take notes, they learn, sometimes they put another tortoise into the enclosure, just to see.

Being an animal dealer is thus a fairly lucrative job, at the start of that century. But human mortality, too, is something else entirely: of the ten children provided to him by his wife, Karl Hagenbeck himself lost five in early infancy. People live differently, and for not quite such a long time.

Twenty minutes after her visit to the ticket booths, Giovanna saw Chahine for the fourth time: in flesh and blood, and from behind. Standing in front of the camel enclosure, he had that curiously inclined posture which Doctor Moro had initially attributed to the weight of his briefcase – a briefcase which today Chahine is not carrying. Giovanna made her way over to him; it had been a good quarter of an hour that she had been trying to work out where she was, stupidly going around in circles, and feeling like she was constantly being watched – the keepers must have laughed up their sleeves at the sight of her going past again and again. It was a relief to have noticed the stranger, somebody with whom she had no particular role to play, and nothing to lose. Suddenly sensing her presence next to him, Chahine straightened up. Without really thinking, she said to him, they're handsome, these ... how do you say it in French, *cammelli*? And Chahine replied that you said *dromadaires,* and in this particular case, Arabian dromedaries, in any event, that's what the sign said, he wasn't an expert in dromedaries himself and didn't know if these particular specimens were especially handsome. They appeared to be in good health at least, he added, staring at one of the Arabian dromedaries that had started to piss, an interminable jet that made a gurgling noise as it hit the ground. Giovanna hesitated, perhaps she should allow this bucolic display all the time it deserved, but then she leaned towards Chahine anyway: I'm looking for, you wouldn't have seen ... you don't happen to know where to find the khulans? A sort of horse, with hair like this? With her open hands she imitated a brush cut, and Chahine replied that in fact he had seen a sort of donkey with a crew-cut mane, like that, and he made the same gesture she had and if anybody had been watching the scene at that precise moment – a keeper from one of the enclosures, or somebody else – they would have seen two humans standing face to face, performing a strange pantomime, hands open on either side of their head. And then they would have seen the woman falling in behind the fellow with no briefcase, who apparently knew the zoo much better than she did.

The khulan enclosure was located in the same section. The keeper recognised the new general manager and gave her a smile which she didn't appreciate, he disappeared behind the barrier leading to the stable, and without even thinking, Chahine found himself following her, and then he was standing next to her, in the darkness, under the fake thatched roof. It took them a moment to make out the thing lying in front of them. The curve of a flank, the tail thumping the straw. It was very hot, and a smell of chlorine, urine and dung hung in the air, of dried blood too and Chahine didn't say anything. The only sound to be heard in the stable was the persistent noise of suckling, the little body glistening, shot through by spasms, its head moving this way and that every now and again, distraught, when it lost the teat. Giovanna cast a furtive glance at her companion. He was lost in contemplation, gazing at the animals, his body leaning to one side, as if he were about to fall asleep on his feet – with a shudder he straightened himself, and pulled up the collar of his coat. It was an elegant coat, she had noticed it the first time, a coat that fell nicely and she herself felt rather elegant that day, so there they were, then, two rather elegant people, standing in the damp straw, in the stifling heat, and Giovanna, no longer knowing quite what to think, almost felt unwell. Fortunately the keeper came over to them and filled the space with words, telling them about gestation, about poaching, then squatted down to stroke the mother, with Chahine following suit. His fine fingers slipped through the hair of its mane, between its ears and puffy eyes and down to its moist nostrils, slowly stroking the creature's muzzle, in rhythm with its exhausted breathing.

This visitor to the zoo in the mid-1920s is striding through a confusing space, a far cry from the controlled harmony of its initial layout. Several of the paths are blocked off due to disrepair and lack of funds. Having lost his way, he'll perhaps be surprised to encounter a jackal on the loose, a drift of water pigs. He'll walk past the repurposed restaurant, now the new Zoological Museum: they've filled it with skeletons. He'll notice the state of the rocks, the cracked mounds revealing the wire mesh framework beneath. Since being taken over by the municipality, the zoo is stagnating like the water in its lake. All they're doing is plugging gaps, battling with nature as it reclaims its rightful place and covers the fake icebergs with moss. Piercing shrieks ring out from the foliage, a branch quivers as a couple of lemurs swing through, the visitor will be advised not to walk under certain trees, so as not to risk staining his hat. There'll be no talk of recent incidents, of the Bengal tiger that tore off its keeper's leg, of the macaque that ate its own hand. That said, there'll be no concealing from him the misdemeanours of Mwana the elephant, news of which will surely have reached him – the animal crushed a veterinarian before strangling its keeper a few months later: nobody understands what happened, it caught hold of him from the other side of the bars, crushing his neck against them.

One would like to say the animals are starting, slowly, to assert their presence. But the animals are not asserting anything, no more than they are questioning – that is a human privilege, and it's the humans who are starting to suspect something. At least the more sensitive amongst them are, the more attentive. The visitor striding down these paths, one fine Sunday in the mid-1920s, is a sensitive and attentive man: he is well aware that this zoo is a sick jungle, a place one comes to die. An institution on the way out, much like the country as a whole, a decadent structure, infected with laziness and lack of ambition. This will all have to change, the weeds need to be ripped out, that mosquito-infested lake cleaned up. Expand, give back to the animals the vital space they are lacking, a deficiency which, according to the visitor, amply justifies the elephant's behaviour.

But it isn't the elephant the man has come to see, that fine Sunday. He has come to visit the young lioness he has been given, a lioness which has now grown, and which has too overpowering a smell – according to his housekeeper – to be allowed to remain in the house. So her cage is opened for him, he enters and the phosphorus flashes crackle as he strokes her, his face serious, his chin held high. Benito Mussolini has learned how to handle the light in his face, without blinking. Tomorrow he will be on the front page of almost every newspaper, because he already has a little power, and soon he will have enough to manage the zoo, and the entire country. His lioness has been christened Italia – in the photograph, she has her eyes closed.

The bar next to the lake was only offering hot dogs, and the doors of the restaurant located at the far side of the zoo had been sealed up. So Giovanna had invited Chahine to the self-service cafeteria at the entrance, which was hardly more appealing but did have a terrace. The sun was out on that early January day, small bright yellow leaves lay scattered amongst the deserted tables. A group of keepers were heading back to work after their lunch break; they nudged each other as they shot looks at Giovanna.

Their trays sat on the narrow table, almost touching. They both started speaking at the same time, Chahine pointed to the window display of the toy shop, Giovanna asked him if he had any children, Chahine said he couldn't decide between a polar bear and an elephant. And then he smiled, replying yes: a daughter. He wanted to buy her a present, a fluffy toy. And what about her? I'd take the bear, said Giovanna, returning his smile. I love polar bears, even if it has been ages since we had any, here that is. I expect they don't cope very well with the climate. Are you on holiday? No, I'm an architect, replied Chahine.

Giovanna waited for him to continue but he didn't, Chahine chased away a pigeon that had landed on the chair next to them, she noticed then that they were surrounded by pigeons, a peacock approached. It's a bank, said Chahine, then, I have to redesign the interior of a bank, but you can only work on it when it's closed to the public, on Sundays and Mondays. Giovanna remarked that it was, in fact, a Monday, and Chahine raised his eyebrows, Monday already, unbelievable how time passes, then he added that the chicken was tasty, but the fries were a little cold. A crow landed noisily on the neighbouring table.

Why don't you come and work for us instead, joked Giovanna, have you seen the state of the place? You'd have to start by redoing this restaurant . . . and then the rest of it. She then shared with this stranger the difficulties she was having to deal with on a daily basis, which was not very professional but was frankly quite enjoyable, and the birds continued to flock around them. Chahine commented on the Great Aviary, which he very much liked, and the remains of other architectural features which they could perhaps showcase, little details that were buried under the vegetation, making the zoo feel like some Aztec city or an abandoned film set. You should see Cinecittà, Giovanna suggested, if you like this sort of decrepitude. Chahine told her how much he loved Italian cinema, quoting names, actresses whose lines he knew off by heart. She remembered having seen them on the cover of magazines, when she was little, and her parents sometimes pointing them out to her, in the street. They were real people for her, older now, their memory a little blurred around the edges, whereas for Chahine they were ghosts with very precise outlines. His favourite director was Antonioni, he added, and Giovanna admitted that she used to love falling asleep at the cinema.

Then there was a lull in the conversation. The zoo's general manager wondered what she was doing there, trying to convince herself that this man represented a new target audience warranting her whole attention. Do you think pigeons eat chicken, she then asked, vaguely preoccupied by the carpet of birds rustling around the table, which Chahine did not seem to see. He had taken out his telephone and was looking at it intently. She didn't dare disturb him, but then yes, she did all the same: I think I have to go back to my office, I'm sorry, do you know what time it is? Chahine apologised, he didn't have a clue, his telephone was completely out of charge, he said, showing her the black screen. It wasn't a problem, he continued, he now knew how to get back to his hotel. They both stood up at the same time, and found themselves suddenly trapped by a joyous whirl of panicked fluttering.

A new wind is blowing across Italy, a wind which is drying out swamps and carving through mountains, which is rushing through city arcades and school playgrounds, and this wind is drawing crowds as it flattens the wheat, and gathers armies at the gates of the Orient. For it is blowing a long way, this wind, it is blowing across the Mediterranean, across deserts and djebels, all the way to the high plateaux of the Horn of Africa, and it is this wind which is making the feather of the black guinea fowl quiver, the feather chosen by Princess Hélène of Orléans, Duchess of Aosta, to adorn her hat. It is the only thing about her that is quivering. Her face is impassive. Her finger, on the trigger, is immobile. A herd of gerenuk is grazing below: she takes aim at the one furthest to the right, the one with its head raised, the one which has sensed something. When it falls, the others will take flight and will be trapped in the beaters' nets, and the most handsome of them will be put into a ship's hold. The Duchess of Aosta's rifle shot marks the beginning of a great hunting campaign. The princes, counts and commanders of Italy dash to the foothills of the Himalayas, to the valleys of Guatemala, to the forests of Sumatra, this one to snaffle up a rare markhor, that one an ocelot, another a spider monkey or an elephant calf, which they can then gift to the reinvigorated zoo. Even Vittorio Emanuele participates in this noble effort: from his domain in Tuscany, the king sends an otter.

In Rome, the institution is undergoing a transformation, driven by a more authoritarian management than its predecessor board. The public is returning to wander its paths, their layout clearer now, and their borders planted with dracaena, hibiscus and weigela. 'Family Sundays' are organised, 'Student Days' and dog shows for the bourgeoisie, all trumpeted by a new media and communications office. Every day a regiment of zealous gardeners gets stuck into pruning, clipping hedges, pulling out weeds. The drainage system is redone, things are cleaned up. Sick animals are disposed of. Ideally, only one pair per species would be retained, a healthy, fertile pair, orders are put in to the governors of the colonies and in reference to that year alone, the year 1927, the archives note:

From Eritrea, one Egyptian mongoose, one African civet, two servaline genets, some jackals, an Abyssinian rock hyrax, one common duiker, one klipspringer, two red-fronted gazelles, one male Nubian donkey, one olive baboon and two Amur leopards; from Somalia, in addition to the Duchess's gerenuks: one yellow baboon, one Cape potamochoerus, one flying fox, one monitor, one python, one oribi, a pair of *Bison bison* and numerous birds; from the Dodecanese, one eagle and two giant salamanders; and from Tripoli, thirteen polar bears. It is possible the archives contain some errors, a few odd inclusions, but one must be mindful that the person responsible for recording the material is facing a Herculean task because from this point onwards, Italy is making an inventory of everything, documenting and recording its progress, for the greater glory of the regime and for the edification of future generations. One couldn't possibly take offence if some survivors from Hagenbeck's time originate officially from the colonies: things are liable to be a little muddled in the enthusiasm to renew and revive, and anyway, Fascist geography has little use for climatic constraints. A wing is added to the museum and an adjective to its name, henceforth it will be both 'zoological and colonial', and tattooed talismans and dried butterflies, urinary vases and deformed skulls, narwhal horns, necklaces made of fingernails and royal jewellery are all haphazardly crammed in, nobody knowing the precise nature of the object or its actual provenance – a fact which subsequently will also avoid them having to be returned. At the entrance to the gardens, a new enclosure is constructed, dedicated to anything directly or indirectly resembling an antelope, and which henceforth will be referred to by a majestic wrought-iron sign as the *Gazelle dell'Impero*. Ostriches are made to parade past.

One week later, Chahine was standing in front of a giraffe, a plywood giraffe, screwed to the wall and measured into segments. The various ages of a human life were marked off along the length of its neck, the height of a child at five years old, at ten years, and so forth. Chahine imagined a world measured by the yardstick of that animal. Such and such a Le Corbusier building would be six giraffes tall, you'd calculate the ceiling height in baby giraffes, the width of doorways in gorillas. Volume would be estimated in the number of seals, and you'd use the graduated markings of a zebra for more precise measurements: you could find animal equivalents for anything, except perhaps for toilet seats which of course had to reflect the precise dimensions of a human backside. That's what Chahine was thinking about as he waited for Giovanna, while the rain pattered down on the shelter. The window pane that gave onto the enclosure was dirty, the animals had withdrawn all the way to the rear, into their Moorish house, and their absence left the space entirely clear for his own reflection, a grey coat and a face with drawn features looking back at him obliquely. He turned away and unfolded the map of the zoo.

The ticket attendant had already given him several copies – and each time he had carefully studied the brochure, disappointed to note that it was still identical to the previous one, and still just as inaccurate. On it, for example, the lake was blue. The enclosures were represented by ovals of grassy green, with round trees resembling apple trees scattered here and there. The paths were yellow, and the buildings an orange colour: it all gave a semblance of unity to a place that no longer had any, a place where one might see the sharp tip of a Teatro del Pinguino appearing suddenly like Corbusier's chapel at Ronchamp, behind a squat, bunker-like elephant house. Only the extension carried out in the 1930s retained its initial symmetry, even if it was now the most decrepit section of the grounds. The buildings surrounding the Great Aviary were covered in moss, their windows were broken, plaster was peeling off the walls of the Reptilarium but none of all this was visible, on the glossy paper map.

Chahine looked up, the little tourist train went past him, in the halo created by rain as it bounces off things: a ghost train driven by some hooded fellow, hunched over his steering wheel. The little carriages were empty, as they had been every time he had encountered it – the driver was paid by the kilometre, evidently, regardless of his load. The last time they had seen it, Giovanna had wondered why the thing was shaped like an old locomotive. After all, it was electric, they could have made it any shape at all, a caterpillar or a spaceship. Chahine had replied that all toy trains sold to children had a funnel. Perhaps it was also an attempt to turn back the clock, as it crisscrossed the zoo.

He would meet her almost every day, and almost by chance, that's to say, around one o'clock in the afternoon outside the giraffes' house. Sometimes she was too busy to come, or else they would run into each other further on, at the pygmy hippopotamuses or the tamandin. The old keeper would then take his chance to tell them a story or two, or three, for example the one about the little Malaysian sun bear that had hidden in the museum restrooms. Giovanna tried hard to translate the colourful tale for Chahine, and the Algerian listened attentively. He liked her accent. She rolled her 'r's, rounded her 'u's, and it's not that it's particularly tuneful, an accent, but it launches you straight into the anatomy of the sounds, the curve of a tongue caressing a palate, the slightly forced protrusion of lips, the suck of saliva – that's what's appealing, about people who have an accent: you can hear their body. So Chahine listened to Giovanna's body telling him how dey had discoverrred de bear cub, de sounde of de washebasins it was tearing offe de wall, de broken water peeps, de inondatzione that had ensued, and the keeper carried right on with a story that apparently concerned his father and a panther – but Chahine was only listening to the music of the words and besides, Giovanna was frowning and smiling as she spoke, it seemed she herself did not understand everything she was translating.

At other times, they would merely listen to the great animal silence. The piercing cries whose origins they would try to guess, between the dense branches of the magnolias. She didn't ask him any questions, and anyway, he would avoid answering. Algiers, the shuttered apartment. When he was with Giovanna, he could forget all that, and the phantoms tugging at his sleeve. But Giovanna wouldn't be coming today, it was a shame, he would have liked to have a sandwich with her, or something hot. These were the most visible things on the map he was holding: big symbols in bright blue indicating a plate and a knife and fork. The letters WC. A figure in a wheelchair. A gift-wrapped parcel. In that respect, too, the leaflet was lying, various shops were closed, as were most of the restrooms. However, despite its shrill optimism and its lack of detail, the printed map held one big advantage over those he could bring up on his phone: he, himself, did not feature on it.

The leader of the government is hunched over the city's maps. He's in a terrible mood on this summer morning in 1927, he has been refused access to his lioness's cage, she is an adult now and it could be dangerous for His Excellency, and His Excellency is infuriated by the caution of his compatriots and the timidity of his ministers. He has also just learned that the Jardin d'Acclimatation in Paris and the London Zoo were both fifteen hectares, whereas his own zoo measured only twelve. The virility of an empire is proportionate to the size of its zoo, everybody knows that: it must be expanded, the grounds adjacent to the eastern side will be annexed, on the other side of the road leading to the Parioli neighbourhood, there are a good five hectares there for the taking. Somebody in the room coughs, nobody dares tell Il Duce that the Berlin Zoo covers an expansive thirty-five hectares.

The extension is entrusted to the architect Raffaele de Vico, the man responsible at the time for Rome's villas and gardens. He is a man with supporters: like any good builder, de Vico is also a mason – he was initiated by the sculptor Ettore Ferrari, Grand Master of the Grand Orient of Italy masonic lodge, and even though lodges have now been banned by the regime, their influence persists. But de Vico is not a mason for opportunistic reasons, he is a man with a taste for the clandestine and for initiation processes, and while his colleagues use their rulers to design white towns crushed by the sun and their convictions, de Vico is building terraces, planting trees and creating shade. He'll add a fasces motif to his fountains for good measure, or some imperial inscription which he designs so as not to have to carve too deeply: he knows the slow work of moss and the cycle of seasons, he knows how the murmur of water can hollow out the hardest stone. He knows, too, that history is the true foundation of art. The young Fascist architects harp on and on about the need for a *tabula rasa,* whereas de Vico is never done with admiring the fruits of the Renaissance, the treasures of Borromini, the coolness created by artificial grottos and the melancholy of broken columns scattered through romantic gardens. He observes, he studies, he distils and blends it all together, searching for hidden correlations. And so, behind the Villa Borghese, de Vico has just finished a water tower, a tower that is at once temple, vault and pagoda. The peculiar monument is connected to the ancient Aqua Marcia aqueduct, but it also incorporates the most up-to-date hydraulic techniques – it is a giant clepsydra and the curious architect knows its every gear and piston, everything which allows the electricity to offset the weight of the liquid. It's with a childish happiness that he listens to the hum of the pumps and, with the palm of his hand resting on the pipes, imagines the water circulating – water which will supply the surrounding dwellings, the park's fountains and the animals in the zoo.

There were only six hundred khulans left in the world. Giovanna knew how to estimate the size of a crowd in any given space off the top of her head, but she was incapable of picturing six hundred donkeys scattered across a Mongolian steppe, of understanding if that was a lot or not very many – the figure meant nothing to her, and there was no chance the birth of their khulan would make the headlines. She had refrained from contacting her most influential friends, but all the same, she had ensured a photo of the newborn had appeared in one major national daily which Moro was holding in his hand. The little doctor appeared pleased with himself, and the director too, but self-satisfaction was second nature to him. Half a page, not bad, said Moro, and Giovanna shrugged to indicate that it was no big deal, at the same time running a hand through her hair, which suggested the contrary.

The doctor remarked that the shot had been retouched, to enlarge the little animal's eyes. Giovanna had no time to protest. Your photographer had the right idea, said Moro, raising a reassuring hand, it works every time, enlarging the eyes, and with its head tilted to one side like that … don't you just feel like picking it up in your arms? It's adorable … but all the same, I think it might be time to move on to more adult strategies. Absolutely, added the director, considering it a timely moment to wrinkle his brow, without having the slightest idea what Moro might be suggesting. What was bothering the good man this morning – in much the same way he might be bothered by a digestive issue or the fact that he was feeling a little peckish, two of his primary concerns – was the call he had just received from London. His counterpart was asking him what was happening with the delivery of the tamandin, they seemed most impatient. Moro shrugged. They had ended up finding a carrier who could take on the job, now they were being held up by customs but Giovanna was dealing with them, wasn't that right? Giovanna raised her eyebrows, there had clearly been some misunderstanding, she thought he was the one who – it doesn't matter, Moro interrupted her with a weary gesture, he would look after it. In any event, the London project was doomed to fail, they had two other specimens over there of this extraordinarily rare variety of anteater, the Endangered Species Convention had resolved to put them together but nothing would come of it. He had just returned from a conference on ungulate fertility in Chester, it had been a complete waste of time. Ever since they had saved the Arabian oryxes, the English thought they could get street lights to copulate. The director gave a chuckle, Giovanna suppressed a shiver. She well understood the significance of the subject, and that the survival of zoos depended on it just as much as the survival of the species. But she couldn't help imagining the animals forced to share a cage, observed by scientists dressed in white, just watching and waiting. It was an entirely personal opinion, she really knew nothing about it, but she couldn't seem to make her peace with the issue: after all, in a zoo, the poor animals didn't get to choose each other. Moro smiled. It was a little more complicated than that, he said, wiping his glasses, and 'choose' wasn't an appropriate term for animals on heat. Even for human animals, a loving choice of partner was nothing but a very recent illusion, and one that was perfectly in tune with general consumerist tendencies. Giovanna herself had not truly chosen her husband, had she, she had simply met him through friends they had in common, or at a concert, or a gallery opening, all within the narrow confines of her socio-cultural territory.

'I think you're underestimating the number of variables a little,' suggested Giovanna, who was not thinking about her husband at all.

'Yes, probably … And yet, how we still cling to our little illusion of liberty, don't we. I've never really understood why. In fact, the probability of two ordinary individuals mating is infinitely higher if they find themselves locked up together. That's the advantage of artificial environments … A little like a man and a woman on a desert island, for example,' the little doctor added, fixing his gaze on her.

Giovanna looked away. She was sitting with her legs crossed, stroking her arm in a solitary embrace, and Moro appraised the contrast she provided to the fat director slumped in his chair behind his desk. She was a beautiful woman, what men would consider a beautiful woman: symmetrical features, a fine jaw line showing no visible hair. Well-proportioned shoulders with a hint of rounded breasts under her sweater. A defined pelvis, insofar as he could judge, femurs converging in tapered fashion, rounded knees, discreetly curved gastrocnemius muscle. A foot was swinging at the very tip of a slender, leather-sheathed tibia. The foot froze when she caught the direction of the doctor's gaze, but the doctor nodded his head. Quite right, he said, consulting his watch, it's already late.

They both grabbed their armrests at the same time, but Giovanna was outside well before the others.

When he is asked to design the zoo's extension, de Vico starts by wandering along its paths. The architect finds it entertaining to see the brown bear performing grotesque Fascist salutes outside opening hours: one keeper has named it Fritz and, unbeknownst to management, has taught him to stretch up its paw each time it is offered a treat. But it's the astounding span of the elephant's feet that de Vico most admires, that and the golden eyes of the Somalian crocodile, the fractal shapes of the Indian star tortoise's shell. The architect was only familiar with mythological portrayals of reptiles, which he has often used to decorate his fountains – so he takes great delight in these living examples, admiring the design of their scales, following their slow undulating movements over the damp earth. The macaws and toucans are more difficult to appreciate, restricted by their rusted cages. Parakeets flit overhead from tree to tree, and crows sketch fleeting imprints as they flash across the sky. How is one to capture this beauty? You would have to build invisible frames for the birds, as vast as air itself. For indeed this is what has been asked of the architect: new aviaries, but also a reptilarium, an aquarium, an elephant house and a children's playground. And he is told, most importantly, to be quick about it.

In 1930, the zoo numbers more than three thousand creatures and those numbers are on the rise. They are fertile years, the Empire's spring, the regime is committed to encouraging love: there are proud celebrations around the birth of great grey kangaroos, brown lemurs, mandrills, Siberian tigers and sea lions – and lengthy press releases are drafted to announce a few world firsts, the litter of Amur leopards, the birth of Victoria the orangutan and Pippo the chimpanzee. Even the notorious polar bears from Tripoli never stop copulating. But the front page of the dailies is reserved for Italia the lioness, who has given birth to three cubs. They want to name them Nice, Savoy and Tunisia; France is up in arms against the invocation of its territories, a portent of future friction, but it is still too early for all that. The matter is thus put to popular vote, schoolmistresses gather up numerous little folded notes, families write in to newspapers and the result is as unexpected as it is unanimous. In one of those demonstrations of collective intelligence that characterise free nations, the three lion cubs are named by the people, Bebe, Nini and Toto.

The old reptilarium is partially converted into a clinic, and the zoo finally recruits its first veterinarian. This obscure predecessor of Doctor Moro also keeps records, the content of which is not always picked up by the authorities. In them one reads about the fate of Victoria, who has died at the age of one following a tooth infection. One learns that the entire chimpanzee family has been carried off by tuberculosis, and that the bears from Tripoli are systematically devouring their young. The vet asks for more work space, they want to give him the entire building but first of all a new reptilarium must be built. So what is de Vico doing? De Vico is sitting at the edge of the lake, de Vico is looking at the trees, de Vico is watching the birds.

The paths often finished in a dead end, in storage areas, toolsheds, condemned sections glimpsed through gaps in the wooden boards: ends of pathways punctuated by stagnant water, invaded by weeds. But Giovanna and Chahine cared little for such obstacles, and on the pretext of carrying out an inspection of the grounds, Giovanna led them ever deeper into the zoo. Or perhaps it was the zoo drawing them into its history.

Thus man and woman stumbled blithely between wheelbarrows and piles of branches, searching for something they themselves seemed still unaware of. They crossed a space which thirty years earlier had been filled with water and penguins – Chahine raised his arm to stroke the enormous ghost of a walrus passing right by them, and he looked so serious as he did so that Giovanna could not have said whether or not it had been in jest. The soles of the man's shoes slipped across the dead leaves, the woman's heels skidded over the mossy slopes of the iceberg – Chahine turned to reach out a helping hand to Giovanna and she caught it with her fingertips, laughing, and they ended up regaining their foothold on the upper terrace, amidst the great white bears, in the ghostly vapour from their nostrils. Giovanna turned back to contemplate the gardens from this high vantage point, perhaps because she was hesitant to continue, but Chahine had already disappeared into one of the grottos.

She should not have been there, in the company of this stranger who might just as easily have cracked her head open with a rock, in the half-light of the bears' den. But for her, fear had never stood in the way of attraction, and in any event, the man did not split open her head: he contented himself with striking his palm against the latch which held the bars closed, at the back of the cave, and the gate opened, creaking, through to a corridor plunged in darkness. Giovanna fumbled her way after the grey silhouette, bumping into things with her boots, hands stretched out in front of her, brushing along the damp walls. A ray of light revealed a cupboard punctured by rust as if made of paper, and Chahine greeted a keeper, that's to say, a keeper's jacket hung up on the wall, under an outmoded cap, the folds of which had been colonised by spiders.

They emerged onto a narrow, scrubby path, a brick wall running along it. Giovanna stopped once more. I can't work out where we are, she said, and Chahine turned back to her, rummaging in his coat pockets. He unfolded a map of the zoo. Together they leaned over it. Giovanna's hair, like delicate antennae, caressed the glossy paper, and Chahine's fingers. It's as if we've disappeared off the map, she murmured, but Chahine lifted his head, looking for some point of reference nearby. Right at the end of the path stood a rectangular build ing, which did not feature on the map.

De Vico, the architect, is still sitting at the edge of the little lake. The weather is fine, he has dozed off, he's dreaming of a rocky island, of a white figure in a small boat, of gently swaying cypresses. But a hand touches his shoulder, waking him up: it's the director of the Zoological Gardens, accompanied by various people of note. They want to know what progress there is with the works, they impress upon him the problems of overpopulation, promiscuity, that time is getting on – good, good, answers de Vico, who stands up with a sigh, puts his hat back on and heads off on a journey.

In 1934 he visits the zoos in London, Berlin, Antwerp and the one in Vincennes, which has just opened. He doesn't learn much from them. In Munich, the zoo is managed by Karl Hagenbeck's son-in-law, a certain Heinz Heck. Munich is the capital of Nazism, its zoo is even bigger than the one in Berlin and it is the first to be divided into large geographical areas, grouped around fauna and flora from similar latitudes. We've calculated the amount of sunshine in each area, Heck explains, we're monitoring the humidity, and conditions are optimal, we have the highest fertility rates in the world. All of this is enthralling but a long way removed from the Roman architect's remit. There's a fierce rationalism raging here, too; in order to facilitate upkeep, fake rocks have been abandoned in favour of sterile concrete: smooth walls, square cages. Deaths resulting from epidemics have fallen by 23 per cent,

Heck boasts, we've eradicated the most common illnesses. He also shows him other things which are of no interest to the Italian: rubbing his hands, Heck explains how he wishes to bring back, through some audacious hybridisation, the wild aurochs and also the tarpan, a horse which has been extinct for decades. The creature which is breathing in the hay does indeed resemble a horse. Its legs are too spindly to allow it to stand upright, but I'm almost there, says Heck, before leading de Vico through to the aurochs enclosure and admitting, when faced with his guest's pallor, that in fact there remains much work to be done on this particular specimen. But they will be true Europeans, enthuses the zoo's director, the wild and pure species which have been part of our civilisation since the dawn of time! Then they spend a little while visiting the rest of the city. Heck shows him the construction site of the Führerbau and the Haus der Deutschen Kunst, which is showing an exhibition on degenerate art and the abominations of the Judeo-Bolshevik avant-garde. De Vico thinks that Cubist portrait there looks a bit like his host's aurochs but he says nothing, manages politely to take his leave and gets into the car which is to drive him to the station. It is while he is en route that the architect notices something above the roofs, something which in the end makes it all worthwhile he asks the driver to stop immediately, there, yes, he gets out and stands transfixed, eyes to the sky, frozen before the formidable building, a gigantic cylindrical reservoir containing the town's gas.

On top of it sits a delicate cupola of metallic lacework, and as a result, de Vico will miss his train.

The building which Chahine and Giovanna had noticed that day was Moro's laboratory. The doctor had seen them approaching, and they were unable to avoid him.

'I expect you're an architect?' asked Moro, shaking Chahine's hand. Giovanna was surprised to hear the doctor speak French, while Chahine wondered, looking down at himself, what it was that could have revealed his being-an-architect. It's the shoes, said Moro, laughing. Well, actually, it was your eyes first … When people walk in, they generally look at the microscopes, the beakers. But you looked up at the door lintel and at the angles of the walls, you only looked where there was nothing to see but cement and air. I suppose you might also be a civil engineer, but I suspect those shoes of yours are a little too fancy for that … English, aren't they? But come, let me show you around, Giovanna has never deigned to venture this far, now's our chance. As you will have noticed, the premises have been repurposed; it used to be a reptilarium, which explains the small windows. At least that means we can carry on with our work away from prying eyes.

Giovanna hated test tubes, the jangle of metal against glass, the smell of disinfectant – it was a visceral thing, the clinical neon light made her feel anxious. An unattractive, hunchbacked fellow was fiddling with pipettes in a corner; he acknowledged her with a sort of grunt. Moro had launched into a lecture about acarids, alopecia in gelada baboons and parasitosis in peccaries – words which sounded a little too apposite, thought Giovanna, words to lull you to sleep, like the rumbling of the large freezers, whose contents she wasn't sure she wanted to know.

Chahine had paused in front of a glass tank lined with newspaper. The shiny orange spiral of a small snake lay coiled in a corner. A convalescing *Pantherophis guttatus*, Moro explained, it had almost been eaten by its brother. The two reptiles had been eating the same mouse, one swallowing it down from its tail, the other starting with its head: at some point, spasm after spasm, the bigger of the two had started swallowing the smaller one; they had been discovered by somebody just in time to pull them apart. But he's doing well now, tomorrow I'm returning him to the vivarium. The keeper is calling him Fortunello. Sweet, don't you think? You see, he added, throwing an amused look at Giovanna, that's one of the advantages of being the mad scientist … while everybody's furiously trying to work out what he's up to, there he is, quietly devoting himself to life's little everyday tragedies. But come through, he said, pushing open a door, it's your lucky day. It's not often you have a chance to see a big cat up close.

The lioness was called Maya, and she was stretched out on the operating table, her eyes closed, a dressing on her flank. Even like that, thought Giovanna, her majestic presence filled the entire room. Come closer, no need to be afraid, said the doctor – and following his lead, Giovanna gently placed her palm on the animal's fur.

She was one of the zoo's recent acquisitions, an Asiatic lioness who had not adapted well. She had started displaying stereotypy behaviours shortly after her arrival, endlessly pacing the same path, over and over again, each step finding her previous pawprints. Every time she went around, she was rubbing her hip against the big window of the enclosure – until finally she had worn off the fur in that patch, creating an open wound. The lesion had become infected and it was not a pretty sight, I can tell you, continued Moro. It must have been very painful and yet she never altered her course. At first we tried putting obstacles in her path, but she always managed to find a way to rub her sore. We ended up having to remove her and place her in isolation, the last few days she even started gnawing at the patch. Sometimes, we can't help worrying at our own wounds, said the doctor, eyeing Chahine over the top of his glasses. But Chahine did not react, he was still looking down at the great beast.

He had held back while Giovanna gently stroked the lioness's muzzle, smoothing her long white whiskers, at once moved and intimidated by that great maw with its closed eyes. As she stroked her cheek, she unwittingly revealed the animal's black gums, and the yellowed ivory of her fangs.

'There's no danger, is there? I mean, she won't wake up, will she?'

'Highly unlikely,' said Moro, smiling. 'She died this morning.'

Back in Rome, de Vico does his calculations, sets out his figures and evaluates spans. He, too, has fitted out a small laboratory, in the house he has been allocated in the northern section of the grounds. He has ordered metal samples, large quantities of acid, receptacles and retorts and sometimes, while things are simmering, he looks out the window. He's keeping an eye on construction of the second gate, which faces the main entrance, on the other side of the road. He's also watching the young women lining up outside the administration building. It's an odd sight: they're all either clutching a moorhen, or have a fennec fox on a leash or a guenon monkey on their shoulder. Gifts which their fiancés have brought back for them, when they've returned from overseas on leave, cute little things which they don't know how to get rid of, now that their fiancés have departed once more. It's 1935, and there are many soldiers on the other side of the Mediterranean. War has just been declared in Ethiopia, and it won't be long before the last independent nation in Africa is conquered. It will allow the capture of a few nyalas, those beautiful antelopes native to the Entoto Mountains, as well as some gelada baboons. The conflict will cost the lives of 3731 Italians and 250,000 Ethiopians, which is a lot for a few baboons, but the gelada is a gracious primate, with its long, curved canines, its lion's mane and the little red triangle which adorns its chest.

De Vico doesn't spend much time thinking about Africa, or about colonisation, he is busy digging a tunnel under Via dei Parioli, to link up the old zoo with its new extension. The passage emerges at a set of stairs worthy of an Aztec temple, passing between two curved buildings connected by a small arch: a gateway to the sky. The steps inspire awe in all who climb them, drawn upwards by the promise of some mystical revelation, and the anticipation of crossing a threshold reminiscent of the Palazzo Zuccari, or the great mouth of Bomarzo's Garden of Monsters. The first thing seen from that height are the labourers busy pouring the foundations, affixing long tubes of sparkling steel, delicately erecting, triangle by triangle, the fantastical dome of the Great Aviary.

The first reviews are unanimous, journalists emphasise that it is the largest aviary in Europe; they even go so far as to compare it to the miraculous vaulted dome of the Pantheon, despite it in fact being its exact opposite. The aviary is sheltering neither gods nor relics; the sole purpose of its transparency is to show off the spectacle of life. It is, by its very form and function, the perfect example of the rationalist oeuvre.

And of course, the reasons for that are many: astonishing as it might seem, de Vico is one of the first architects to notice that large birds are reluctant to turn at right angles, and that it would be preferable to allow them a generous, circular flight path. But his aviary is not just the result of calculations, it is also the fruit of a curious hybridisation, the marriage of an Indian star tortoise's carapace and a building in Munich, one of those mysterious fusions which even the architect himself probably doesn't realise. De Vico is equally unaware that his skills as an alchemist have led him to discover an alloy that will survive the century, resisting every thermal variation – when Chahine sees it, from the balcony of room 324, the polyhedron is as shiny as the day it was constructed, with not a trace of rust.

No time is wasted in filling the handsome frame with Peruvian pelicans, black-crowned cranes, African sacred ibises and a couple of Andean condors. The birds themselves are not at all interested in posterity; the only thing which matters to them is the current and inescapable matter of the mesh in which their beaks get stuck. Far below them, milling around, is an assortment of hats – top hats, flower-bedecked hats and soft felt hats: it's time for the official opening ceremony already. Dignitaries are entertained by the dazzling flash of wings, and by the squawks from the smaller adjoining aviaries – people offer their opinion, comment on the pretty children's play area, admire the new bandstand and the little orchestra performing a few Saint-Saëns fantasies. And then the orchestra makes way for a choir of uniformed young people singing the praises of the Roman eagle and Italy's flight towards spring.

Next the guests head down to the Reptilarium. Its doorway is the dark twin to the aviary's entrance: a mouth framed by stucco serpents that leads into the shadows.

On that particular day, the ghosts remained at the entrance to the Reptilarium, and Chahine went in alone. He liked this place, the heavy heat of the air, the darkness, the smell of earth that caught in his throat. De Vico had designed a circuit that wound its way around a central pond, and Chahine made his way slowly up the ramp, past the vivariums set into the adjacent walls. The murky water weighed against the panes of glass, an iguana pushed its foot up against the window, dragging its claws across the glass. A kingdom of serpents, where silence ruled. The buzzing of a flickering neon light. A slimy swirl in the pond water, a few undulating reflections.

Following his visit to the laboratory the previous day, Chahine was on the lookout for the little orange snake, the one that had been christened Fortunello after being pulled, in extremis, from its brother's mouth. Moro had explained that its heart had stopped beating, just for a moment, and that it had required cardiac massage and a dose of atropine to restart it. Chahine wondered if the little snake retained any memory of those seconds, of the moment when, just as he was enjoying the mouse in his own mouth, he had started to suffocate in the mouth of his brother.

A turtle from Bengal was floating, perfectly still, its head poking out of the water, its neck severed by the refraction. Its heart, explained the information panel, beat only 28 times per minute. It was tempting to infer from that its perception of things, to form a picture of its universe: an elongated world, dilated and muffled, like a sound recording played at reduced speed. But a minute means nothing, to a turtle. It scarcely has any meaning for humans either, beyond the rules and conventions of clockmakers – for there are some minutes when the human heart beats 70 times, and others when it climbs to a pulse of 90, and then there are some minutes where it beats 180 times, when the blood rushes through the arteries, pounding in the eardrums, and one might think that time is accelerating for a man pumped full of adrenaline and spurred into action, but that would be a mistake. On the contrary, beyond a certain point, time baulks and crystallises, slowly – and the moment is forever engraved in the neural networks of his encephalon.

Chahine was searching for the small orange snake as one might hunt for oblivion. He was fruitlessly scanning the miniature landscapes, one after the other, when he heard steps. He turned. Giovanna was walking slowly towards him, brushing the wall with her fingers. Her eyes had grown wide in the darkness, and suddenly she was there, very close to him.

The Reptilarium closes in 1940. There is not enough fuel to maintain it, indeed there is a lack of everything, except mouths to feed. The consequences start making themselves known: the peregrine falcons are spotted fighting over the remains of an amethystine python, or sea lions are seen feeding off the flesh of a blue iguana. The Genoa Zoo has just been bombed, so a few survivors have been taken in; a distraught, quivering snow leopard, a Nile crocodile, a tamandin and a few African penguins. But it's a struggle to find adequate foodstuffs, even on the black market, and the zoo is forced to bring in the same self-sufficiency measures that have been implemented across the entire country. Small plots of earth are cultivated wherever there is room, two cows are brought in which are not entered on any register: they will ensure the youngest animals, along with the keepers' children, have milk. In summer, pine nuts are carefully collected in the shade of the umbrella pines, and in winter, acorns are gathered around the grounds.

In July 1943, the death of a little egret is noted: the San Lorenzo neighbourhood is devastated by bombs, a miniscule piece of shrapnel manages to make it across the city, penetrate the Great Aviary and strike the small bird on the head. It's all very upsetting, management also laments the considerable decline in visitor numbers: from 308,000 tickets in the first half of the year, to 68,000 by the year's end, no doubt due to the civil war that has just broken out following the armistice. When the wind blows in the right direction you can hear gunfire in the distance. People are hungry. The keepers are starting to eye off the animals with curious looks, and when the two rhinoceroses die as a result of inadequate food supplies, nobody dares ask after the fate of the bodies.

As a precautionary measure, the most dangerous animals are removed to the small coastal town of Sabaudia, at the same time as Mussolini and his ministers are banished to Salò. The big cats are treated well by the German occupiers: keepers are allowed to use a car from time to time to go looking for the carcasses littering the countryside. So when the Americans then land at the little port, they are astonished to discover the great beasts caged up and for the most part well nourished. There's an ageing lioness called Italia, and a Marsican brown bear they call Fritz. The soldiers find the bear hugely entertaining: whenever he is offered a sweet treat, the hefty creature hauls itself onto its hind legs and extends its arm – it's so funny they keep making him do it, over and over again, until the animal collapses, stuffed full of sweets.

A grey light filtered into the room through the curtains. It lit up the sheets on the unmade bed, the heavy red and gold armchair, the rocky landscape hanging on the wall over the television. It was shining, too, on an immobile body, lying on the carpet in the foetal position. You'd have to lean in very close to make out the movement of the man's breathing from under the coat covering him. There's an empty beer can not far from the body, standing neatly upright on the floor, and the crumpled wrappers of two chocolate bars. Every day, somebody would come to the room to clean it and leave some more food, it was quite handy. The minibar offered a limited choice, which the man found practical, rather than a nuisance, and the items of food were always put back in the same place, sometimes two of each. So in the evenings, the man would eat chocolate bars and every now and again, for a change, he would open a tin of peanuts. That morning, the grey light was also illuminating a small bottle of prosecco sitting on the dressing table. The light was being refracted by the glass, casting a rainbow rosette onto the lacquered wood, its shifting curves an imperceptible marker of the passing hours.

That same room could have been described quite differently, for example in the form of a few figures in an accounting ledger, entered under travel expenses. One day, in a developer's office, somewhere in Riyadh, some employee will pay close attention to those figures. He'll wonder why they're still incurring the daily expense of a hotel room in Rome, Italy, when the relevant contract ... let's see, Rome, concept study, project contract ... yes, as suspected, the supporting agreement terminated some time ago: an agreement duly rendered null and void, as is often the case when one of the two parties no longer answers the telephone. But for the time being, it was lunch time in Riyadh, the accounts ledger was closed, and the guest in room 324 had simply decided to extend his stay, for a job he was utterly incapable of carrying out. The bellboy would meet him in the corridors with a beaming smile, and when he emerged from the lift, the receptionist would greet him with the usual deference – that particular morning, he merely glanced quizzically at the lobby clock, for Chahine had come down much later than normal.

Giovanna was also struggling to throw back her sheets. Her husband had tried to rouse her when he left, but she had waited for him to close the front door before opening her eyes. First she consulted her phone, to delay the moment when she would have to get up and also because she had heard it vibrate several times when she was still half asleep. There was evidently something significant going on, the screen showed two missed calls from Moro, who never normally called her. And there were also three voicemails. The first from somebody very agitated, although terribly British – she couldn't make out a thing that was said, except that it had been left by a journalist who was insisting she speak with her. The other messages were from a German number, and the English was thus far more comprehensible to an Italian woman who was still half asleep. It was the animal freight transporter, the one who was supposed to be responsible for the anteater. His truck had left Hamburg the previous day, he had already made it halfway, he was near Innsbruck, when somebody had called him, from Rome, to cancel the job: we require written confirmation, the voice was saying, you can't just reverse the order like that, from one minute to the next, especially as the job's already underway, please contact us at your earliest convenience. The freight transporter's second message was much less polite, and much longer: the London Zoo is insisting the transfer be completed, my truck is not going to do thirty-six round trips down the A13, it's sitting in a motorway rest stop at over a thousand metres altitude and it's carrying sensitive material which is in the process of freezing, not to mention the driver and the vet travelling with it, it's unacceptable, disrespectful, code of ethics, should they head down to Rome yes or no and then the voice mentioned a contract, damages, but Giovanna was no longer listening, she was in the kitchen, busy spreading a fine layer of Seville orange marmalade on a slice of toast.

She called Moro as she left her apartment, didn't get through, and then, in the lift, listened again to the message left by the English journalist. This time she thought she could make out something about an epidemic, but she certainly didn't see how that could have anything at all to do with her. She fixed her hair one last time in the large mirror in the entrance hall, and smiled. It had been a while since she had last worn earrings.

Unlike the Berlin Zoo, the zoo in Rome has never had to witness the slaughter of its animals, nor has it ever closed. Certainly, many of the families wandering through in the late 1940s have suffered a loss, a husband, a father or an uncle, but life is slowly resuming and the real damage is still to come. On 2 May 1949, an extremely handsome collection of antelopes arrives from Somalia. There are gerenuks, lesser kudus, spiral-horned antelopes, proud East African oryx and even little Grimm's duikers. But on 4 May, the kudus start foaming at the mouth, and the next day some of the gerenuks are lying dead on the ground, and there is concern for the other recent deliveries. The new arrivals are isolated in the quarantine area and tests are conducted, as their limbs start to tremble and their eyes start weeping pus – and now, just as the results come back, a baby giraffe chokes on its tongue, on the far side of the gardens. They realise they are dealing with an ancient and terrible thing, that initial precautions have been inadequate to contain it – the keepers themselves have facilitated the spread of the disease, carrying it in the folds of their clothing, between the hairs on their skin. Rinderpest proceeds to decimate the zoo.

The head keeper, Leonardi, rubs a hand over his face. The gesture takes only three seconds, but it allows him to block out the world completely, it helps, it's what humans do on average thirty thousand times a day when they blink.

Leonardi, however, is not a man to regularly cover his face, he has done it only twice in his life: once when his wife cheated on him with a wine merchant, in the autumn of 1936, and once when told of the death of Fritz the bear, when Italy was liberated. But he mustn't dwell on all that, thinks Leonardi, readjusting his cap, now we have to think about protecting the entire city from the epidemic. The gardens are cordoned off, *carabinieri* are posted at the entrance gate. The director has managed to end up on the right side of the gates just before they're closed, so it's up to him, to *capo-guardiano* Leonardi, to take responsibility for the quarantined zoo. He feels like he is on a ship lost on the high seas, a ship where he has suddenly been made captain.

As for the other staff, they're in for a nice holiday: they'll be with their colleagues, they'll sleep in the animals' enclosures, they'll go back to gardening in their clandestine little vegetable patches. They'll play cards. There's nothing more pleasant than a zoo with no visitors: much like Leonardi himself, all the keepers are the sons or grandsons of farmers, and all of them harbour an innate mistrust of the city slickers in their Sunday best who are usually there wandering along the paths, with their polished shoes and parasols and their white collared children, the same children who always end up throwing stones at the peacocks, and spitting at the monkeys. The keepers are accordingly much more at home on the other side of the bars, passing the time with the mute creatures in their care.

Then the order comes to slaughter them. Nobody is allowed to assist the keepers because of the quarantine, and there are still a good two hundred ungulates in the gardens, including the giraffes, the red river hogs, the Libyan Barbary sheep, the Indian gayals and the American bison. The keepers don't know how to go about it. Obviously, a few of them learned how to use a firearm during the war; what they don't know how to do is kill animals whose births they have witnessed, animals they have named and fed, and whose smells they recognise, just as the animals recognise theirs when they come to see them of a morning, greeting them with a word and a bucket of fruit. So it's Leonardi senior who takes on the job, with the help of his son, a lad of twenty-seven, who would also rather be somewhere else.

Gunshots ring out for four days straight. The other animals are very agitated; it's the smell of blood. From the city centre, great plumes of smoke can be seen rising into the clear sky.

That is how Europe's last rinderpest epidemic was brought to an end. When the old keeper recounted the episode to Giovanna, he used other words, coloured by his Roman accent, and by details only he knew. Not that he himself had witnessed the epidemic, but he had been born in July of that year, in 1949, during the quarantine. His father was just a young keeper at the time, he had often told his son how he had scaled the fence to get to the maternity ward that night.

But all of that is in the past, *tempi passati*, said the keeper, looking at the tamandin. Both of them were in its enclosure waiting for the zoo's director, and for Moro. The creature had taken cover behind its bush, with just the tip of its snout and the husky sound of its breathing discernible. Giovanna asked if she might approach it, but the keeper replied that it was a timid animal, and its claws could be dangerous. It's quite a sight, to see Oscar suddenly rear up on his hind legs. He has only done it to me once, but that was back in the beginning, when we didn't know each other yet … Normally he's only active at night, sometimes he'll even go for a climb in the tree. But these days that's rare, he's getting on now, like me … In any case, I'm very happy he's not going off to London, added the man, running a calloused hand over his face.

The silence that had settled between animal and humans was interrupted by the insistent ring of Giovanna's phone, which she didn't feel like answering. She was cold. She was also ashamed, not to have paid more attention to this creature, now it was about to become a curiosity. And suddenly she realised this very simple fact, that in the rush to sell the spectacle of so many different animals, how easy it was to forget the fascination conjured by the presence of just a single one. Moro had told her that when observing an animal one should first take note of its tracks, and Giovanna shivered to see the deep gashes etched into the tree trunk. The enclosure was tainted by violence and solitude.

The keeper cleared his throat. I'd very much like, he said, in a hoarse voice, I mean, if it's possible, I've already asked the *dottore*... I'd very much like to keep looking after him.

That evening, Giovanna fronted the press conference. The epidemic affecting the London Zoo had claimed the lives of two tamandins, two armadillos and one okapi. Tests were being carried out but authorities from the British zoo were saying that the epizootic disease had been brought under control. Moreover, they were insisting the transfer of Rome's tamandin go ahead as previously agreed, particularly as their infrastructure was, in their view, best placed to deal with the animal. Rome had flatly refused; international authorities considered that in the absence of reproductive possibilities any such voyage was utterly pointless.

To the question of knowing whether they really were dealing with the last living member of the species came the reply that the disappearance from the wild of this species of anteater had been confirmed for some time – to the best of their knowledge, Oscar was indeed the sole surviving tamandin. The chief scientific officer, Guido Anselmo Moro, intervened to clarify that in any event, this was the only specimen able to be observed, and that was what mattered. He then answered a few questions about the life expectancy of the *Tamandinus tubulidentatus,* or pearly anteater (fifteen years or so in its natural habitat, twenty in captivity, and Oscar was already twenty-three), about its diet (mainly ants, termites and fruit, sometimes he was fed polenta). One distracted journalist asked about the gestation period, prompting chuckles around the room. A few photos were then passed around, and measurements given. Comparisons were made with its nearest cousins, the aardvark, with which it shared a common habitat and diet, and the giant anteater, from which it differed in the reddish colour of its fur and the scaly plaques running down its back, from skull to tail – a comprehensive information pack would be sent to those interested.

At the end of the conference, Moro asked Giovanna why a press pack had not been prepared, why refreshments had not been provided, and moreover, where was the director. He appeared anxious, he didn't think there had been very many journalists – even fewer than when they had announced the birth of the khulan. Giovanna shrugged, perhaps when all was said and done, people preferred a good news story? The doctor threw her a pitying look. No, the problem was that the media suffered from a woeful lack of imagination, and they hadn't yet woken up to this. And who was that woman in the suit, sitting at the back of the room? She had missed the tour and then hadn't said a word the whole press conference. Giovanna told him she was an editor from *World of Animals*, that she had come straight from the airport, and she didn't speak Italian. Did he want to look after her? Take her to see Oscar? She herself struggled with her accent. And no doubt you have better things to do, said Moro, noticing the man in the grey coat waiting at the doorway. They're pretty, those earrings, you should wear them more often, he added, before going over to the English journalist, with what Giovanna considered to be a peculiar spring in his step.

Giovanna and Chahine made their way through the corridors of the administration building towards the exit, and a little woolly monkey flashed past them at top speed. Only Chahine noticed it, just as he was the only one who saw it slip under a secretary's desk. She was busy typing out a purchase order in duplicate and the monkey suddenly appeared behind the typewriter, snatched the carbon copy, which he rather fancied, scrunched it into a ball and proceeded to munch on it, indifferent to the secretary's exasperated cries. This is what Chahine described to Giovanna as they walked along, and she laughed at his imagination, for she was unaware of the fact there had indeed been a secretary in a pencil skirt in those very offices in the mid-1950s, along with a woolly monkey and numerous other creatures, to greater or lesser degrees domesticated.

Chahine could see all this just as clearly as he was able to see Giovanna, which explained why he would sometimes swerve oddly to avoid an aquarium that had however been long since removed, or a pot plant that had withered half a century ago now – but at the end of the day, it was all quite amusing, and anyway, even the most well-suited lovers don't always see the world in quite the same way. Giovanna simply thought the handsome man walking alongside her was completely mad, a matter about which she was mistaken: he was still only half mad. Just then the zoo's former director, the late Armando Scarelli, emerged from his office – his hand brushed past Giovanna's hip, and no doubt his hand would have lingered there had he been able to see her, for he was known for chasing skirts, and in particular, the tight-fitting skirt of his secretary. He was better known still for his expeditions to the Amazon, for his talents as a photographer and for his constant need to be surrounded by animals, which was as true for the time spent at his office as the time he spent at home: at that very moment, a spring evening in 1957, his wife is giving a bottle to a baby orangutan that Scarelli has brought home from the zoo because it has been rejected by its mother. Knowing that the monkey is in good hands, Scarelli is in the clear, and it is with glossy hair and languorous gaze that he gets back to his secretary, who is still busy chasing the woolly monkey and what remains of her purchase orders around the office.

So she's in a very bad temper and not at all in the mood for this; she rebuffs the director's fingers which are already fiddling with the buttons on her cardigan and Scarelli is forced to suggest they first take a walk, go for a wander around the Villa Borghese in the setting sun and eat an ice cream, to which the young woman hastily agrees. Everything feels more comfortable outside, far from those offices which smell of monkeys, of reptiles and big cats; outside you're in the city, taking in the air with other civilised beings, people who have the power of speech and a taste for the finer things in life, and this is just what Giovanna thinks too, teasing Chahine as they walk through the Aurelian Walls and down Via Veneto. Has he visited Rome before? The Forum? The cafés and museums? But she stops before she asks him why not, so as not to spoil the moment, so she might simply drink in those dark eyes, sipping a sugary-looking aperitif. It is perfectly possible to enjoy an aperitif while standing on the edge of an abyss; you just don't look down, you drink and talk of other things, allow the inebriation to creep up on you – Giovanna stands up and holds out her hand to him and he allows himself to be led, down the gentle slope towards Piazza Barberini, to Via del Tritone and the Trevi fountain, carried along by the joyful click-clacking of her shoes and her laughter when her heels slip between the cobblestones and she catches herself on his arm, and they beat a path through the tourists, take the steps down to the burbling water and whinnying horses, there are so many people about, especially for him, because now he's seeing double, perhaps they will also see Scarelli and his secretary in her pencil skirt, but Giovanna scoffs at the idea. Now she feels like kissing Chahine, at the edge of the fountain and in the anonymity of the crowd, putting her hand to that already tingling cheek, kissing him fully on the mouth and pressing her body into his – and Chahine buries his face in her ash-blonde hair and closes his eyes because there, in the bubbling waters of the Trevi fountain, over Giovanna's shoulder, he has just spotted a sea lion.

In the early 1960s, the zoo does indeed take in a sea lion that is discovered in the Trevi fountain – it's a rare Mediterranean monk seal, to be precise, that some reveller has brought back from Sardinia on a wager or to make his friends laugh, who knows. In any event, Director Scarelli is delighted. His wife is threatening to leave him and his secretary threatening to resign but his collection of animals is expanding from one day to the next, his zoo is packed with celebrities and the whole city is scrambling to see them.

Take, for example, the lions Quo and Vadis, gifted to the zoo by Metro-Goldwyn-Mayer. They've been seen devouring Christians on the big screen, in the eponymous film shot at Cinecittà, but to think that Quo and Vadis are also direct descendants of the MGM mascot, George, the lion who roars majestically at the start of each new company production! In any event, that's what the agent had said when he came to offer the creatures to the zoo – in actual fact, they used more than eighty lions to film the scene in the arena and after the filming, there were Quos and Vadises to be found in most of the zoos and circuses of Europe. But that is neither here nor there, in a world where Nero speaks English and the colosseums are made of polystyrene: anything goes, and all that matters is the angle of the light.

Now there's a big bright sun shining down on Italy, and the zoo is playing host to one continuous party. Giorgio the chimpanzee gets hard every time he sees a blonde walk past, claps his hands whenever anybody says *Forza Roma*, and pokes out his tongue if they say *Forza Lazio*. The kids love annoying him if they can find any sticks long enough. No question they're taking their lead from the head keeper, Leonardi junior, who valiantly slips a rod into the open jaws of Carlo the hippopotamus in order to show off the span of his jaws, before tapping on his teeth like a xylophone, to demonstrate his resounding good health. Shouts of laughter chase each other down the dusty paths, children clutch fistfuls of peanuts, ride the carousel for ten liras a turn, before being handed a bag of anchovies and when they've finished using them to bombard the walruses, they watch, wide-eyed, as enormous blocks of ice are slipped into the water to give the polar bears some relief from the Roman summer. Their daddies bring them to see Romoletto dance, the great-grandson of Fritz the Fascist bear, while their mummies go off to ask intimate questions of Anatole, the Human-Robot, an attraction specially brought in from Paris which is completely fluent in Italian.

The zoo is so popular you're likely to run into the Queen of Jordan or the Shah of Iran as they take their time wandering around – or Salvador Dalí, who's busy pretending to paint Tommy the rhinoceros's horn for the benefit of some journalists. The gardens attract numerous actresses too. On the occasion of every birth, a ribbon is tied to the gates of the zoo, white for the males, pink for the females, and Scarelli invites some starlet to be godmother to the tiger, bear cub or ocelot. They bravely venture behind the grilles to hug the cute little fur balls and pout at the photographers, or boldly toss a birthday cake into Carlo's jaws, or sit side-saddle on Remo's rough back, kicking their legs, laughing and throwing kisses to the crowd. These are just some of the images which appear in the cinema newsreels. Ahead of the Saturday night feature screening, between a visit from President de Gaulle and a handshake between Khrushchev and Nasser, one might also enjoy a few fashion shoots in the gardens: a swimsuit parade in front of the pink flamingos, a festival of fur coats in front of the leopard enclosure. In the voice-over, the master of ceremonies will be comparing the colourways, the stripes, the markings, the walk and, ever the philosopher, will conclude that *women and felines are endowed with all the same virtues, and share the same adorable flaws.*

The next morning, Giovanna spent an hour biting her nails alone in her office. And another hour scrolling through religious images on her screen, rereading the story of Saint Anthony the Abbot. A painting by Velázquez portrayed him with Paul the Hermit who was fed by ravens, his grave dug by lions – it was Saint Anthony who taught him the art of the retreat, which he will then implement by disappearing into the Egyptian desert, fleeing his increasingly numerous disciples, and the temptations of the Devil. Amongst so many others, Flaubert had written about him, and Dalí had painted him. But what astonished Giovanna was the omnipresence of animals in this myth. While they were, from time to time, portrayed as allies of the Almighty, they seemed more readily an embodiment of Evil, meting out the most varied of torments to the poor hermit, his body tortured by their jabs and bites, his mind haunted by their nocturnal apparitions.

It was not a sudden passion for African recluses that had her trawling the net, but rather the visit, in precisely twenty-five minutes' time, of a priest who was coming to bless the zoo's animals, as was the custom every 17 January on the feast day of Saint Anthony the Abbot. He had ended up becoming the patron saint of animals, and in particular, of domesticated and farm animals – which is to say, the 'good' animals, thought Giovanna, the ones who had submitted. In the countryside, however, the feast of Saint Anthony had long been known as the night when the animals would talk – at sunset, you were supposed to steer a wide berth of barns, stables and forests, for it would bring bad luck to overhear the creatures conversing.

She had spent enough years at the city's municipal council to know that it was perfectly normal for Rome to entertain rituals from some bygone era, so it was perfectly normal for the man of the cloth to burst into her office, decked out in a richly embroidered stole and an ostensibly benevolent smile. Off they went to the elephant enclosure, accompanied by the director and a cameraman. Twenty or so people were already there, Giovanna scanned their faces looking for somebody she couldn't find, and the ceremony began. The director read some passage from the Scriptures, stumbling over the words; he reminded his listeners that God had created every beast of the earth and every fowl of the air, and that He had had them approach man so that man might name them – and the elephant, who was called Remolo and who was swinging his trunk behind him, waved it higher and higher and ever more vigorously, and at *behold, God saw that it was good*, the elephant exhaled noisily. The priest smiled: Remolo had shown the same enthusiasm last year, don't you remember? he asked, stepping prudently away from the moat. And then he asked one of the young lads from the gathering to hold up a small goblet, said something about the salt of the earth, and took a little salt from the cup, tossing it onto the ground. There the little crystals remained, glittering on the cold cement, pointless and sterile, thought Giovanna. Then the priest took the holy water and symbolically sprinkled it over every creature in the zoo, and also, less symbolically, over the closest onlookers and the elephant behind him, causing an increase in the frantic trunk swinging, which the keeper was unable to calm down. Grace was hastily said, the spectators made the sign of the cross, a few photos were taken.

Before everybody dispersed, Giovanna suggested to the priest that he accompany her to the enclosure of the last tamandin. It was, by definition, a unique opportunity and not one he should miss. The man was about to decline quietly, for he still had other services to lead, when Giovanna started speaking to him about Saint Anthony. She had a question that was really bothering her, she claimed, as she slowly started to walk off: why was the Devil always portrayed with a tail, hoofs and horns? While improvising some learned response, the priest was forced to fall into step with her – and his entire little entourage along with him.

The tamandin's territory had been expanded that very morning, with the neighbouring cassowary having been moved out. But the little creature remained hidden in his corner, behind his favourite bush. All the same, people had read the newspapers: thirty-odd visitors were gathered at the fence, all trying to catch a glimpse of it, to which now were added these latest arrivals – it was thus quite a crowd which the cameraman, at Giovanna's instructions, was rushing to immortalise within a tight frame. It was the perfect image of visitors pressed up against each other, telephones held at the end of outstretched arms. There wasn't a sound to be heard, the onlookers held their breath. Giovanna heard the squeak of the priest's patent leather shoes by her side, as the poor man stood on tiptoe, discreetly trying to make himself taller.

Success is always a matter of alchemy. Italy has celebrated the centenary of its unification, which means the Zoological Gardens have tallied up half that number, taking full advantage in the wake of those celebrations. For it too was in need of a bit of money: neither the smiles of a few actresses, nor Armando Scarelli's ambition, would have been enough on their own. Unfortunately, it's not long before we've seen the last of Signore Scarelli. While heading up the Rio Negro on his umpteenth photographic expedition, the zoo's director leans over just a little too far. A man of many virtues, he does not however know how to swim. People try to help but he's thrashing about – after much spluttering, his body starts its slow descent, gnawed upon by red-bellied piranhas, arapaimas and toothpick fish. Back on the surface, Armando Scarelli leaves a more or less grief-stricken wife, and more than three thousand animals in captivity.

Municipal councillors descend on the institution to argue over its reputation. Management falls within the purview of the Heritage Department, the Department of Parks and Gardens, along with Youth and Sports Services, all of whom have some difficulty agreeing. Nobody knows who should decide what anymore, management structures are questioned, it's a sign of the times – directors are replaced in quick succession, none of them is a zoologist, all of them have grand plans. The elephant house goes up, the one de Vico had not wanted built, it's in the shape of a large, circular blockhouse, and it constitutes the final blow to Hagenbeck's legacy. An audacious penguinarium is erected, with a soaring roof line reminiscent of a Corbusier cathedral. The building should have been the world's first penguinarium, but it is never opened: once construction has finished, they are unable to bring in the machine to run the cooling equipment. A year later, in 1963, it's the Reptilarium's boiler which explodes. Apparently, it is quite a complex task to re-create micro-climates in a space the size of a pocket handkerchief, and is it really all worth it? The Communist municipal council has the costly institution in its sights.

The film industry also spurns the Zoological Gardens. At Cinecittà, the euphoria of historical epics has given way to the cynicism of the spaghetti western, from time to time a python makes an appearance, or a tarantula, but only as props – they have more need of pistols, horses and thin-lipped actors, and the zoo can't help with any of those. Or if they can, it is by complete happenstance. In the autumn of 1966, a black *Panthera pardus* escapes from its enclosure, sowing panic amongst the visitors. Augusto Leonardi makes a dash for the locker room, where he grabs the Winchester M1 Carbine rifle – his arms recognise the weight of the weapon, his fingers recognise the warmth of the butt, and suddenly the metallic smell takes him back seventeen years, because this is the weapon that was used to slaughter the bovids during the plague. It is still perfectly serviceable, and when the shot goes off, Augusto thinks of his father.

Actresses stop venturing to the zoo. The public abandons the gardens, and enclosures start to rust. A thick layer of moss covers the moats, the greenery planted in more prosperous times is left to grow and the vegetation explodes, camphor laurels, areng palms, ginkgo trees and other still more peculiar species, the seeds of which have been carried in the fur of creatures from Asia and elsewhere. There is no botanist to embark on any study of this new jungle. Once evening falls, the keepers' children gather up feathers in the aviary to make themselves Indian headdresses.

Giovanna sets off down the paths, she is unsure of her step because only the animals are illuminated, and each animal is picked out, frozen, in a beam of blue light. Somebody is singing in the distance, an old Neapolitan *tarantella*, a wolf watches her and Giovanna quickens her step for there is no fence between them. Further along a shrew is asleep, its tail disappearing into the darkness, she could get her bearings if she were to follow it, she just has to walk along next to it, making sure her foot keeps brushing past it, so as not to lose herself. Moro tells her that it isn't enough, that it's all very well but it's not well thought out, and in Giovanna's dream, she hears him say the word 'thought' in French, and she notices that the little man walking next to her has stuffed his ears with cotton wool, and that frightens her. The doctor suddenly points out a brick wall that has been taken over by ivy, you see, I told you so! A giant moth is hovering against the wall, and she wonders how it got in, because now they're in an enclosed space. And then she sees a second one, crawling along half-heartedly, stuck to the wall, and others are following it, they're scarcely moving but Giovanna realises they're looking for somewhere to be, she sees the moths are now covering the entire wall and are forming a message, symbols tumbling over each other, changing as they shift – a message the gist of which she struggles, upon waking, to recall. All she remembers is having grasped its significance.

By the end of the 1960s, Romans have good reasons not to go to the zoo. Most households have a television set: it's a considerable investment and the fathers of such families decide to get their money's worth by remaining in front of them. It's all the more pleasant as a supplementary invention has spread across Europe, attributable to one Edward Lowe, from Michigan and now a multimillionaire. The inventor of kitty litter. It has allowed the proliferation of a new breed, the apartment cat, and it has the great advantage of sitting quietly on your lap as you pat it, while you watch TV.

The small screen offers up the most extraordinary things, places you would never have set foot. And so, on the evening of 13 October 1974, viewers of the first station on Italy's RAI television network are able to admire the plains of the Kilimanjaro and their infinite skies. In the documentary the sun rises over an idyllic scene where, according to the narrator's voice, *the scent of man is still a far-away thing*. And then we see the scent of man approaching at top speed, with a growling of motors: the camera is plunged in amongst the tyres of a 4WD, its lens blinded by dust, the giraffes in the distance have already set off at a gallop but the vehicles are gaining ground, they catch up with the animals, and a well-thrown lasso strangles the slowest of them, yanking it to the ground while the men – a few black men, not many whites – jump out to immobilise it, tie a blindfold over its eyes, lift it back up and push it into a narrow crate.

We have to act quickly, explains the hunter, mopping his brow, so the shock doesn't bring on a cardiac arrest or lung infection. Similar scenes follow, the capture and poaching of a zebra, an ostrich, and a few images from an acclimatisation area where trembling antelopes are tranquillised for weeks on end. Next we are shown the inside of a container littered with fruit, and then piles of containers being shunted onto vehicles and taken to Nairobi, before being loaded onto rust-coloured trucks heading for Mombasa – and this is where the aeroplanes take off, says the narrator, where the freighters take to the sea.

According to the documentary, an estimated one hundred million animals are forcibly removed from Africa every year, bringing in six billion dollars. When the crates are opened, there's often not much that remains alive inside (or to be precise: one monkey out of every eight, one bird in fifty). But there are several prospective purchasers for those which do survive: zoos, circuses, laboratories and especially individual collectors. And then we learn that in Europe it's all the rage to have an ocelot on your terrace or a python in your living room, and the thoughtful viewer strokes his cat: 80,000 liras for a giant Madagascan flying fox, it seems reasonable enough, all things considered, and it's almost enough to plant the seed of an idea. On the small screen, a rhinoceros is shoved into the hold of a Boeing aircraft while the humans take the stairs; the final credits run over the image of a plane taking off, against a soundtrack of simian shrieking.

Which brings us to the end of part one of Riccardo Fellini's documentary, *The Mad Zoo* – yes, he's the other one's brother, but it's not something he likes to be reminded of. His thesis is that all animals in captivity are deranged, that they have been irrevocably sent mad by the trauma they've suffered. Staff at the Rome Zoo are not yet alive to his intentions when Fellini shows up to work on part two of his documentary; his team is warmly welcomed by the director and by the keepers, and also by Giorgio the chimpanzee. Every day Giorgio performs a little number for the visitors: he smokes, hangs from the bars, bares his teeth, and good naturedly turns it on for the filmmaker's camera. But when Fellini's back is turned to film the public, Giorgio creeps up behind him without making a sound, snatches Riccardo's hand from between the bars and rips off his index finger at the first joint with his teeth. Fellini is bleeding, a little pale, but delighted, because this bipolar behaviour perfectly illustrates his theory. The chimpanzee keeper, for his part, is distressed, he grips his cap in his hands, murmurs that you should never turn your back on an animal. He also mumbles an explanation which nobody hears, in the brouhaha that follows. Maybe Giorgio was simply jealous of this man who got between him and his audience. But it's an era in thrall to science: rather than accord a monkey the capacity for emotion, better to saddle him with a healthy psychiatric dysfunction, something able to be endlessly measured and observed. The Fellini documentary thus gathers several choice sequences: African wild dogs pacing in circles, bears shaking their head, birds flitting frenetically backwards and forwards from branch A to branch B … A mother leopard that devours its newborn's belly, tits that destroy their own eggs with their hysterical pecking … Ibex mounting each other all day long, masturbating rabbits … A bleeding, depressive gorilla constantly pulling out its own hair, baboons banging their heads against walls.

The night of the televised broadcast, the zoo's director explodes, stamps his foot, grits his teeth, threatens to destroy his living room furniture and takes it all out on his wife: he feels betrayed, manipulated by the odious editing. All those behaviours have a perfectly rational explanation, he claims, gesticulating wildly – but it's too late to demonstrate that now. Households across the land are shaken by Fellini's film and, from one day to the next, Italy finds itself at the forefront of the anti-zoo movement.

In the hushed environment of the administration building's waiting room, Chahine sat dreaming. It was the fifth time he had come, but the concierge didn't appear to recognise him – he was no longer particularly young or very tactful, this concierge, he wasn't used to receiving strangers and so made no special effort for this one. These days, it should be said, there were constant interruptions, the telephone was always ringing in his lodge, and there were so many more comings and goings to interfere with this stolid employee's routine: you could even say that in the circumstances he had remained relatively polite, gesturing Chahine towards the waiting room, and relatively patient when Chahine refused to go in. The Algerian feared he had been misunderstood; he explained again that it was Giovanna he wished to see, and not the large sofas in the waiting room – but the old man was unshakeable and in the end Chahine had given in.

The room had wood panelling halfway up the walls and a few posters had been pinned up, doing a poor job of disguising the damp patches. There was a questionnaire lying on the marble coffee table which Chahine ought perhaps to have filled out, had he been given a biro, as well as a stack of magazines, probably animal-themed. And a calendar, already displaying the month of February. All in all, it was a perfectly pleasant room. You could easily fit a hippopotamus in here, thought Chahine, two even, if they were positioned at right angles, like the sofas. Through the window he saw a forest of giraffes pass by, it was quite beautiful, there must have been a hundred or so of them, they made the light outside blink, and the whole room flash. His daughter suddenly asked him why he had mud on his shoes and he closed his eyes to chase away the image. Then he noticed his shoes were indeed dirty, as was the hem of his trousers. His feet had been very warm for days now, he could feel his socks, wet inside the leather. It's like having your feet inside an animal, Chahine thought, looking at his shoes. Like having your feet inside a calf, and that reminded him of that hole-in-the-wall place where he used to eat in the kasbah that served *head of the sheep*. That's how it had been written on the slate board in chalk, in capitals, after the tagine – exactly like that: not *sheep's head* but *head of the sheep*, as if the dish were an offering, a ritual sacrifice. He had wanted to order that dish for a long time but hadn't dared. In the end he had mostly just found it difficult to eat, that big skull with all its nooks and crannies.

In the 1970s, the ethologist Desmond Morris notes that Western youth like sitting on the ground, which he says constitutes a revolution in human posture in the urban environment. At the entrance to the zoo in Rome, you can also see young women on all fours: they're naked, made up to look like big cats and locked in narrow wire cages. They're surrounded by a horde of young men chanting slogans and brandishing placards, some have climbed up the metal railings and are swinging their arms about, screeching like monkeys. Salvatore Leonardi tries to skirt around the protesters, looking for a way through to the zoo's entrance. He turns his face, probably to avoid having to look at the caged girls, or at least so he only has to see them out of the corner of his eye. He finds them disturbing, these cat women with their painted nails, play-acting, and falsely submissive; he would gladly free them if he weren't so timid, if he didn't have to go to work, if he weren't a zookeeper. They haven't noticed him yet, he slips through to a service entrance held ajar by a colleague – barely has it closed behind him when fists and insults rain down on the other side of the door.

Salvatore is not that much older than these activists, he has long hair like them and trousers that flare wide as an elephant's foot. And yet he doesn't understand them, and the feeling is entirely mutual. They're fighting to *free the animals*, a cause which seems a little too complicated to him, or perhaps far too simple. Two years ago, on a summer morning much like this one, he had come across a large *Hippotragus niger* as he'd been heading back along a path, a sable antelope staggering and bloodied, that kept butting the fence of its enclosure. But it was *on the outside*: somebody must have left a gate open the night before, and the animal had found its way out – for hours and hours now it had been trying to get back into its enclosure, repeatedly beating its horned skull against the fence. It wanted to get back to its own space, and Salvatore remembers the rivulets of blood seeping through the black fur, its exhausted movements, its big black eyes bathed in blood.

His grandfather's Winchester still takes pride of place on the locker room wall, it has been kept as a souvenir, for decoration, or simply because nobody has ever thought to take it down. Much like how he came to be a zookeeper, force of habit, passed down from father to son and without too much thought. Below the weapon, in a glass case, is a new shotgun fitted with a hypodermic syringe. We know now how to capture an animal without inflicting the slightest pain, but it's hard to explain that to people, and harder still when you don't quite believe it yourself. But Salvatore keeps his doubts to himself, because to betray an entire lineage of Leonardis would be unthinkable. He laughs at the jokes of his colleagues who are imitating the protesters mimicking the monkeys, and who make all sorts of suggestions as to what could be done with the little caged tigresses. But if you were observing the young keeper's movements, you would notice he gets changed much more slowly than the others.

His father would sometimes return to the house still dressed in his uniform, to surprise the young lad, and the child would be awestruck. In his schoolboy drawings he would always depict his father in his cap, with his golden buttons, a net in one hand, rifle in the other. At once gladiator, hunter and tamer, that's what a zookeeper was, and his father was head keeper. Now his father was old and Salvatore would rather not wear that hat, not slip on that jacket, not be booed when he crosses the path in front of the gate, under the gaze of protesters hanging from the railings.

Usually he would set off on his morning rounds ahead of the first visitors to check there was nothing to spoil their experience, no greasy wrappers, or any ostrich that had died overnight. But today there's no point, no visitor would dare breach that wall of protesters, so Salvatore heads straight around to the back of the ibex hut, where he's drying his cannabis buds. And then he goes off to find young Guido. He's the only person Salvatore dares confide in, because he's not employed by the zoo: Guido is a young student from La Sapienza University, whose professor has given him the job of observing the tribe of thirty *Macaca fuscata* just received by the zoo – a gift from the city of Oita in Japan, to the honourable city of Rome, Italy. Guido has been recording the interactions of the little monkeys for two months, and for two months, when he has an hour or two free, Salvatore sits on the ground amongst them, in the shade of the eucalyptus trees.

Salvatore likes listening to Guido and his words, even though he only understands half of what he says, perhaps because the student seems too young to be expressing such thoughts, or perhaps because he speaks as if on a stage, without really addressing him directly. Young Guido says the protesters are like the wind, he says the wind is turning, that the days of society as spectacle, of its zoo-circus-cinemas, are over, that the wind is shifting and blowing through the tree tops, and that now is the dawn of a new era, he declaims, making a note that F3 is coming over to present her rear to M14, the dawn of a new era and that the zoo is an Ark, a fortress designed to preserve genetic capital, far from human folly and from the destructive human appetite for accumulation; Guido says the dykes are about to give, as he notes that F23 is delousing F16, the dykes are about to give and the world's markets will come tumbling down one after the other and Salvatore takes a drag, his head is spinning gently and he's never sure if it's the weed or Guido's words, he really does talk too much, and Guido's words end up soothing him like the murmuring of a stream. Salvatore leans back and watches the eucalyptus leaves dancing. Of all those words there is one which makes him dream more than the others; it's the word Ark, because it's a word that gives meaning to his uniform and allows Salvatore to imagine himself as a captain, or midshipman or even just a non-commissioned officer, it doesn't matter which, the Ark just needs to be steered into safe harbour and that's what he'll be able to tell his children, if one day he has any. The wind is turning and the whole zoo is changing course, and MD4 leaps from his branch, and pretends to chase M7, and M7 pretends to flee, baring his teeth.

Behind the bars of the gate the activists are also playing at defying the police. They're beating their chests and brandishing their fists, and the police are beating their truncheons against the bars. Unlike the macaques, who always stop in time, the men will soon come to blows. It's the 1980s already: the streets of Rome smell of tear gas, but also of gunpowder and burning. Weapons are slipped into processions, bombs go off in squares. Small groups of extremists are on the increase, all of them brag about being infiltrated by foreign powers. The new Animal Liberation Front is another group that thinks violence is necessary, they quote the example of Giorgio the chimpanzee: he had to bite off Fellini's finger to make humans change their attitude towards animals. One night in September 1981, protesters carry out a ram-raid and break through the zoo's perimeter fence. It takes several days to repair the hole, and stray dogs make the most of their chance to go in and devour a few ibises.

Salvatore Leonardi is now convinced of it: while his forebears did their best to train the animals, his own view is that it's the humans who need educating. Day after day, he's constantly asking visitors to respect the animals who are guests there. To refrain from tossing coins into the crocodiles' water, to stop throwing cigarette butts into the hippos' pond, to stop feeding the felidae. In the Reptilarium, every second window is empty, which doesn't stop visitors frenetically tapping on every one of them, hoping to catch a glimpse of something. In an attempt to distract them, Leonardi starts telling them stories. He has come to understand the power of words, ever since a student told him that the zoo was an Ark, and the word Ark restored his pride. The other keepers don't always look favourably on his expansive nature, but Leonardi shares all the anecdotes he himself has heard with anybody who cares to listen; he talks about Noah, he pilfers from Aesop, he describes Hagenbeck and how the zoo came to be. He draws on the whole history of the place, repeating the tales of his grandfather, his father, their colleagues. And from time to time he makes up his own.

Here he is, for example, in March 1982, standing in front of the Andean condors' cage. He's surrounded by children, arms spread wide, cap askew, and his lips are vibrating as he mimics the sound of a twin-engined aeroplane – he's imitating a Savoia-Marchetti S.55, the first transatlantic production model: this was the machine on which Giulietta, the female condor, arrived. The minister of aviation himself had gone to fetch her from the Santiago Zoo in Chile, on Mussolini's orders, because Il Duce wanted to make a gift to his new aviary of the world's biggest bird. Salvatore then lowers his arms, and hangs his head. He describes poor Guilietta's loneliness, how she'd been separated from her Romeo, he mimics Romeo's fury in the Santiago Zoo and how one stormy night the raptor escaped, how it had taken flight into the Chilean skies, launching itself after the metal eagle, how it had flown over mountains and waves, its beak aimed at the horizon, and now Salvatore furrows his brow and beats his wings, ever more slowly, he's weakened by the distance, the headwinds and storms, but finally, finally, Romeo makes out terra firma, and lands, half dead from hunger, on the beach at Ostia. The keeper then straightens up and, with a drum roll, steps aside to present to the children the two venerable birds. Perched on his branch, the male buries his moulting head into his collar. The female stretches out her neck to snaffle up, from the dust, the remains of a rat. The children break out into applause.

Amongst the spectators is a little girl called Giovanna. She's eight years old, with pale blonde hair and wide-open eyes. She doesn't applaud, her arms have stiffened at her sides, paralysed at the sight of those enormous black shapes – the female towers over her from its great height, and with a crack the creature opens its immense wings and all of a sudden, it's as if night has fallen, as if the world were disappearing. Moved by the little girl's emotion, the keeper runs a calloused, reassuring hand over her blonde hair, her plump, trembling cheek. Neither of them will retain any memory of it.

The little train could no longer follow its usual route: having made it as far as the pygmy hippopotamuses, its path was blocked by visitors, and it was forced to toot its horn until people noticed and stood aside to allow it to pass. The process lasted five minutes and everybody was annoyed – the Bangladeshi driver who was paid to steer his train around, rain, hail or shine, the public, who had paid to see the last tamandin, and the old keeper, who was trying through it all to maintain some peace and quiet for the animal – people were growing very agitated, and over the brouhaha clanged the trying notes of the train's musical horn.

Giovanna suggested they change the route of the train, which was still a firm family favourite. Moro, on the other hand, proposed they get rid of the fairground relic. The director, for his part, was in firm agreement, but with whom, exactly, it was impossible to say. He congratulated himself at length on the growing number of ticket sales, on the pedagogical value of his institution, on the excellent material that had been shown on the evening news, and so on and so forth. Giovanna then mentioned a new restaurant on Via Veneto, a Sardinian place that did an excellent *zuppa gallurese,* Moro nodded enthusiastically in agreement, the place had a good reputation, but you had to get there early if you wanted to find a seat. They promised to join the director as quickly as possible, as soon as they had sorted out a few technical details.

Moro waited for the door to close before bringing his chair closer, and unfolding a map. They had to move Oscar, he had been considering the matter for a number of days now. There was only one area that could both accommodate his spectators and offer 360-degree visibility from a sufficiently safe distance. I thought, said Giovanna, that animals didn't like to move. True, said Moro, but what bothers them more than anything is if their keeper changes. As long as old Leonardi continued to look after Oscar, the tamandin would soon get used to it. They would also transplant his bush, to make sure the animal would have somewhere to shelter. Most of the birds would remain in the Great Aviary but even so, as a precautionary measure, they would move the marabou and pelicans; their moods could sometimes be unpredictable.

She'd been taken aback by the plan, but Giovanna had nothing precise with which to reproach him. It just felt presumptuous – but she chose to use another word, she called it 'premature'. She had contacted her friends, every media outlet had published the information she had provided, but all the same, she felt as though the story was struggling to find traction. You couldn't gamble the house on a temporary attraction, on an animal that might die the next day. But perhaps that was what was drawing the visitors, and it was definitely an opportunity that couldn't be reproduced – she winced at her unintentional pun. Moro didn't answer, he only smiled, and she realised he'd thought of everything, that their discussion had been merely a matter of courtesy. Still, she did manage to retain the little train.

Every young person from the northern suburbs had done it at least once: scale the fence at night and smoke a few joints in the muggy air of the zoo, to experience the delights of transgression together. But memories of those nocturnal escapades had blurred over the years, and Giovanna had better memories of another visit. She's about fifteen years old and strolling along with a boyfriend, Alberto. Their parents have lingered a little behind, and the teenagers have ducked down a side path and hidden in the bushes, to do what exactly, they're not really sure, but sensing they should be doing it alone. They're crouching down in there, Alberto snickers and Giovanna says *shhhhh* a little too noisily, they elbow each other, not yet knowing how else they're supposed to touch each other – and then suddenly Alberto freezes, and points something out to the girl. She looks up. The bamboo around them is covered in names, clumsily carved into the green stalks, names on a slant, coiled into a heart, crossed with an arrow. A forest of paired names.

That's what the zoo was for, at the start of the 1990s: it was a great, untamed green space, free to be written on. To carve your name, like Giovanna and Alberto, in the trembling silence of their hiding spot. To tell stories, like Salvatore Leonardi. And so what if that little love affair only lasted one summer, if Giovanna would end up sharing her first kiss with a boy called Niccoló. And so what if the mythical Ark was taking on water at every point. What we commonly call reality only really means something to animals.

Giulietta the vulture is sixty-one years old when, beyond anybody's wildest dreams, she offers up a gift, and the gift lies there, perfectly white, in the dust. The male vulture, Romeo, proudly shakes his crest, and the keeper who discovers the egg cannot believe her eyes. Giulietta has not laid a thing since the 1940s, and it is now 1993. Unsure as to how to congratulate the birds, the zoo's management goes to great lengths to congratulate themselves: we must be doing something right, they say, clapping each other on the back, they carry the egg to the lab, they set it down in an incubator and call their friends at the university. A few professors arrive with their assistants: you would recognise Guido Anselmo Moro amongst them, he's wearing little round spectacles, has an already receding hairline, and through his little spectacles he's carefully scrutinising the humans gathered around. He's amused by his colleagues' hysteria, he understands that to them this egg represents the zoo's last chance and that, in fact, they are completely desperate.

These are the darkest years the zoo has ever known, despite its sunlit paths. Light has bleached the information panels that stand askew in front of rusted bars; they're not read by anybody anymore. From time to time they've been corrected by hand, the name of one animal struck through and replaced with a scrawl by another. The last polar bear has been dead a long time and lizards flit across Hagenbeck's iceberg, slithering into cracks in the cement. The Great Aviary is overrun with ryegrass and nettles. The shadow of a solitary giraffe moves slowly across the decrepit walls of its shelter.

Children's laughter is rare, even on Sundays. You can hear flies buzzing and leptospira bacteria swarming. There's the sound of hammer blows from the old elephant house, through the half-open door a keeper can be seen repairing his *motorino*, others are leafing through a newspaper or smoking as they look on. Every now and again somebody might find an article which they read out to the others: there's always some eminent visionary setting out their previously-unheard-of views about a zoo of the future, a natural sciences city, a zoological collection constructed from *CD-ROMs*, a virtual garden with *holograms*, *interactive kiosks* and a giant antenna to transmit educational, *multimedia* and *interactive* programs *via satellite*. The keepers have a laugh at the words; as far as *new technologies* go, they're still on watches with liquid crystal displays and an integrated calculator. But nor are they fools. Well do they know that if there's not enough money to repair feeding troughs or to prune hedges, there certainly won't be enough to install giant screens.

Salvatore Leonardi spends his afternoons in old Giorgio's cage. The chimpanzee struggles to stand upright, he has to be hand-fed and Salvatore cuts his fruit up into tiny pieces, tells him stories which the monkey listens to with his cloudy eyes, and Salvatore keeps talking to him long after he has fallen asleep. Sometimes Alfonso, the son of the entrance café's manager, comes to see him and brings him a macchiato. Is it true they're going to close the zoo? the boy asks, and Salvatore bursts out laughing a little too loudly, Come now, what makes you think that?

The fact is that an ecologist, Flavia Fontanarosa, now has a seat on the municipal council. As a young woman, Flavia would happily lock herself up in metal cages to protest the caging of animals. These days you would no longer recognise her, it's not so much that she has aged, it's more that power does peculiar things to people's features, it has a habit of drawing down the corners of the mouth. But her intentions have remained unaltered: Flavia Fontanarosa has adopted four poodles, she feeds the city's cats, she has become a spokesperson for mistreated animals and, according to her, the Zoological Gardens are their chief persecutor. So she slashes the already anaemic budgets without so much as batting an eyelid, she does her best to strangle the institution. She enjoys the support of her party, the Anti-Vivisection Alliance, the Anti-Hunting League and the Raptor Protection Society. The Turin Zoo closed in 1987, Milan's in 1992. And on the morning of 4 June 1993, after observing the condors' egg one last time – a smooth, white and perfectly silent egg – the zoo's veterinarian decides to turn off the incubator.

The tamandin's transfer took place at night. Giovanna had been anxious to be there, her work kept her at the zoo until all hours in any event. She'd taken social media by storm, just as she had when working in politics, and hours had gone past without her even noticing – the little notifications were still flashing before her eyes as she left the building and plunged into the darkness. It was cool, the wind had picked up and the trees were quivering, and she hurried towards the light shining at the end of the path.

She arrived too late, and Moro did not so much as glance at her. In the halo of a floodlight, two men she didn't recognise were removing the crate from the enclosure, the old keeper following behind with short steps, mumbling something that sounded like a lullaby, their shadows playing across the ground. They set the crate down on a gurney which in Moro's view was too small, he became angry, rain was forecast and time was of the essence – they pushed the large crate along, trying to hold it straight, the keeper was still humming as the thing lurched its way over the bitumen, wheels squeaking dreadfully, the first drops starting to fall, and as they emerged from the underground passage the crate slipped. A curse slipped from Moro's lips, he hissed out orders between gritted teeth, together the men hoisted the crate up, and they started the ascent of the long set of steps. Just at that moment the heavens opened.

It was like a summer storm, rain that had held itself back for months now poured down, in the middle of February, with the violence of a monsoon. Raindrops hammered onto the lid of the crate, blinding the men carrying it who were tentatively feeling their way up the steps with their toes, and their hoarse breathing blurred with the rattle of the water. Moro was flanking the porters, he was shouting. Leonardi had doubtless gone ahead, Giovanna could no longer see him, she was stumbling behind the crate and the crate seemed to be smoking under the rain, she thought she heard a cry coming from within, a whistling, she wished she could do something but she couldn't see anything either, her hair was glued to her forehead – she ended up hurtling back down the steps to take shelter in the underground passage. There was a torrent now running down the steps but the men held steady, the crate continued its slow upwards path, before the silhouettes finally disappeared at the top of the staircase, veiled by the downpour.

Giovanna made it back to the administration building at a run. It was only as she pushed open the door, dripping and out of breath, that she noticed the lights, in the waiting room.

She threw her coat onto the coffee table and crossed her arms to pull off her soaking sweater, but having lifted it up, she couldn't then extricate her elbows. Chahine wanted to say something but she interrupted him in a muffled voice, help me, so he took her by the waist, kissed her exposed neck and tried to undo the buttons on her blouse, arm twisted, elbow jutting out from the mass of their bodies, hand crushed by her breast pressing against him – at last she managed to free her arms, took the man by the nape of his neck, devouring him with a kiss, Chahine again tried to speak but her tongue blocked his words, pushing them to the back of his throat, they fell onto the wide sofa, her fingers slipping under fabric, looking for the warmth of his skin as her long hair cascaded over his face, caressing it like snakes. He bit her shoulder but she pushed his mouth away with her open palm, then he lifted her up by the waist, tipping her over, together they battled the damp, clinging trousers, she was shivering now and nestled up against him, undoing his belt, releasing him before pushing him back so she could stretch out over him, she slipped an arm around his neck and stuck her foot into the mouth of one of the hippopotamuses, pushing against its thick tongue, supporting herself, so she could better open herself up to this man who now wanted to enter deeper still, a bison had burst out of the wall and was looking at them, he thrust his hips, lifting her up into the air, she cried out and the bison made a lowing sound in response, some monkeys had pushed their heads through the walls and were watching the two bodies, entwined, battling, and how dearly Chahine would have loved to open the woman's belly, open it up and pull apart her ribs, tear back her skin and dive all the way in, dive down deep and disappear at last.

Rain battered against the window panes. Water seeped in between the frames and slowly darkened the walls. Eels writhed on the glistening floor.

The Ark is nothing more than a wreck that has run aground on the shores of the Villa Borghese. It would take a magic trick to set it afloat once more, which is precisely what happened, because at the time Italy was living a fairytale and anything, absolutely anything, could happen. What we are about to recount takes place on the outskirts of Rome, because that is where the zoo's fate is playing out: along a side road, the name of which we won't mention, for that would enable identification of a restaurant which must also remain a secret.

A long, black car is in the parking lot, its paint work displaying the glinting logo of an establishment claiming to be a *Pizzeria, Grill and Nightclub.* The muffled beat of techno music can be heard from within – a beat which, on entering, becomes frankly deafening. Lighting is subdued, tables are red, lacquered and empty, there's no pizza being served at this hour. Three men are sitting at the bar and a woman is standing on the counter. She's dancing, her nudity is a momentary distraction and then we notice the thing hopping about next to her: a child in a dinner suit wiggling about, coming and going between the glasses and ashtrays. He's sporting a tie and cufflinks, the curious proportions of its body have us thinking now perhaps of a dwarf, before it turns to look at us with its black, hairy smirking face, its crushed nose and its chimpanzee gums. For the first-timers, it creates quite an impression, for everybody else, it's just Bunga, the venue's mascot. But of more interest to us is the large one-way mirror behind the bar, and what is taking place behind it.

In a corner of the little private salon, a man is on his feet, hands behind his back, and his generous build is not, one senses, intended for the hospitality industry. Two other fellows are seated on a dark purple sofa, the shorter of the two eyes the bubbles in his glass, the other one has crossed his legs and is listening attentively to what the woman seated opposite him has to say. Flavia Fontanarosa is taking a considerable risk in coming here. She is insisting that Bunga the chimpanzee be removed from this frightful place. Yes, she agrees not to close down the zoo, but on condition that it also be used as a refuge for mistreated animals. The man understands everything she says, and also what she does not say, he is used to that. He answers that he knows lots of mistreated animals, more precisely that he knows people who know people, etc. Baby elephants in illegal circuses, domesticated tigers, he can provide her with as many as she would like. And get media coverage for the lot of them. The woman says she's still unsure. I'm not, says the smaller of the men, picking up the bottle to refill the three glasses, should we bring Bunga in? You know, he just adores champagne. The councillor frowns in disgust. She likes the idea of saving a chimpanzee, but the thought of actually having it on her lap makes her nauseous. For her, too, animals are first and foremost words: she replies there's already a gorilla in the room, that there's no point bringing in another one. The men laugh, the bodyguard remains impassive and on the other side of the glass, the chimpanzee claps its hands, rounds its wrinkled lips, attaches itself to the dancer to lick her knee, it has no idea what lies in store.

The official announcement is made in August 1996, when everybody is at the beach. The old Giardino Zoologico di Roma is a thing of the past, it's a victory for Flavia Fontanarosa and her party. The revamp of the wildlife park will be carried out by a public limited company: the company, Cosmo, will hold a 35 per cent share, the Cressi group will take 14 per cent and the municipality will keep 51 per cent, all is well. But the contract contains some fine print. The municipality will continue to be liable for operating costs for another five years. Two representatives from each partner will sit on the board, effectively giving the private stakeholders a majority. They will control the choice of contractors, construction companies, maintenance companies, suppliers and restaurateurs. One clause written in even finer print provides for their exclusion from any liability arising out of such management issues. It is what one might call a particularly juicy deal, but there were many others of its kind at that time, because in Italy those were magical years.

Roman families can remember the opening of the new Parco Natura, in the spring of 1999. Posters are plastered up throughout the city, with smiling monkeys and purring lion cubs and there are few who know what lies hidden beneath these benevolent images. The company, Cosmo, has started by laying off all the old employees, who are fixed up with positions in other council departments: younger dynamic staff, motivated by job insecurity, are preferred. Salvatore Leonardi has found an empty chair in a forgotten office, deep in the bowels of the Zoological Museum – the museum has remained in public hands and is run by the council, no doubt because it is too educational and not sufficiently entertaining, which is to say, it's never going to make a buck. Salvatore is in his fifties, he doesn't really know where to put his jacket, what to do with his hands. He wanders through the corridors, surrounded by animals he knew when they were alive. He remembers them when they were hungry, thirsty, when he used to be able to do something for them. Sometimes he talks to these stuffed bodies, when nobody is watching him. But he never goes over to the windows looking out to the park. Down there they've taken on a young American director, and a twenty-year-old German vet. They seem mostly to have employed people in communications. They've given the zoo a makeover, starting with its words: the Parco Natura now offers a Valley of the

Bears, an African Savannah, an Archipelago of Macaques and many other magical areas.

At the park's entrance, for example, you'll find the new Flamingo Lagoon: a pool in which phenicopters paddle about in the open air, it's an ideal way to welcome visitors because pink is the colour of happiness. People are entertained by the sight of these vertical birds, they think they have a comical walk. Nobody notices that their feet get stuck between the over-sized pebbles, nobody knows that their wings have been clipped, to stop them flying away. Further on, the macaques are still fighting on the same cement hill, and the advertised archipelago is just a word that appears on the new information panels, the pretty, brightly coloured panels with their large type. There is a gulf between what people think they are seeing and the tragedies actually unfolding before their eyes. Families coo over the lemurs with their striped tails, people envy the little monkeys lazing about on a green lawn, in the shade of an umbrella pine. They don't know that the trunk is electrified, and that the monkeys miss clambering on the bars of their old cage. Too bad if they're now bored to death. The humans found the bars really too depressing.

So, railings have thus been replaced by panes of glass, it's an era keen on all things smooth and transparent, it feels like a department store, it's reassuring. The animals, though, proceed to bash their heads against these other-worldly walls, before scratching at the partitions and the odourless shadow dance of reflections. For the glass prevents the animals from smelling the humans, and the humans from smelling the animals: by interrupting the air movement, they have also done away with the age-old apprehension of potential confrontation, of risk. Never before have people been so far removed from the creatures as they are now they're able to hold up their hand against the palm of a chimpanzee. And visitors point out to each other the reclusive thing in the corner of the enclosure, do you remember? He was in the news, it's Bunga, the monkey that they freed, he spent ten years in a nightclub, poor animal, apparently they used to dress him up. Bunga is slumped against the wall, one arm held up over his eyes. He can't bear the other monkeys, or the sunlight.

But to take all this in, you would have to move slowly, take your time, but look, there's a new attraction going past, a little blue plastic train, it's electric and shiny, and you can hop on so you can go even faster, so you can make sure you couldn't possibly get bored, or pay too much attention. So you won't stop in front of the Andean condors' cage, who have not so much as laid another egg. Instead of the large chunks of carcass which once upon a time they would be left to dismember, their meal now consists of small cubes of pressed pink meat.

The visitors, however, are satisfied. The kiosk on the lake has been repainted, it's now called the Oasis Bar, they serve a large selection of vacuum-packed sandwiches. The children are more excited by the toy store, it's brand new and you have to go through it if you want to leave.

Giovanna was leafing through a catalogue of promotional products: keyrings, pens, rulers for schoolchildren, little colourful notebooks. All they needed was the shape of the tamandin on them to sell at ten times their usual price, a fact she was trying to impress on the toy store manager, who was shaking his head, doubtful. Did he know, Giovanna persisted, that the balloon-seller at the zoo's entrance was already offering these? She set a plastic figurine of an anteater down on the table. It was an ordinary Brazilian anteater, but some poor sod had painted a green line down its spine, to make it look like the last specimen. He's selling it for 10 euros, she said, he can't keep up with sales. The man crossed his arms and shrugged his shoulders, mumbling something about the balloon-seller who shouldn't even be there outside the zoo, about immigrants, residence permits and other words she preferred not to hear.

She had a meeting scheduled with the graphic designers, a new agency that had been engaged to redo the brochure – at least they were in the right business, Giovanna thought, heading back to her office. She felt a bit deflated when she saw the couple waiting for her. The girl had a shaved head and the boy was sporting a long double-pointed beard, and Giovanna felt very inclined to judge people by their appearance; it was that sort of day. They started off, using affected gestures and deliberate words, by presenting a graphic chart for which they had opted for a 1930s font style in a range of lolly pinks and electric blues. Giovanna didn't have time to look for a new agency – she explained to them patiently that she was after something more simple, in natural hues for starters. The couple exchanged a knowing glance: their concept, they explained in unison, was that a zoological garden was the most artificial place one could conceive of, and that they would rather keep earthy, ochre colours for the animals themselves, which would make them stand out – they pulled out a first draft of a map, where goose-poo green shapes stood out against a fluorescent background. Only the tamandin was white – white being a colour of *positive mourning*, according to them – rendering the animal almost invisible against the garish background. Giovanna wondered whether they were too intelligent to do their job or if they simply had bad taste. They settled on some drastic changes, they agreed a time to meet again.

On leaving the zoo, she was hailed by the balloon vendor. He opened a big box covered in Chinese characters, from which he proudly pulled a sample: a soft plastic animal which, this time, was an exact replica of the tamandin's anatomy. If you pressed its belly, a retractable tongue emerged from its long snout. Fifteen euros, said the vendor in English, holding out the object to her with a broad smile, but for you it is present. Also new balloons, five euros, look! A dozen big, plump, rust-coloured anteaters floated overhead, swaying gently in the wind.

It had been over a week since she had last seen Chahine.

Six months after the opening of the Parco Natura, on the eve of the year 2000, Giulietta the condor falls off her perch. Her companion follows suit a few weeks later, and the newspapers give a lyrical description of the last flight of these great birds. Large photos are published illustrating their wingspan, the story is told of their arrival under Mussolini, seventy years of history is recounted as witnessed by the raptors, perched side by side behind their bars.

The death of the couple is put down to their venerable age, but in a cellar in the northern suburbs, members of the Animal Welfare League don't see it like that. They have just received an anonymous letter which suggests the birds died of hunger. The letter also refers to the case of Iago the leopard who died the previous year, and says management would have had it euthanased on purely aesthetic grounds, because of its mangy tail. These are just two examples, the letter notes. The Animal Welfare League starts digging into the institution's recent past, and unearths a significant number of cadavers which went undisclosed over summer. The task is an arduous one, because management at the Parco Natura has mislaid the former zoo's records, and they have to rely on a variety of different sources to compile an inventory of deaths. But they manage to draw up a list of seventy-five deaths over the last six months, the first page of which looks like this:

04.04	*one baby yak*	*?*
09.04	*one Bactrian deer*	*cardiac arrest*
11.04	*one hamadryas baboon*	*?*
15.04	*one pygmy hippopotamus*	*† at birth*
16.04	*one red kite*	*?*
22.04	*one llama*	*stomach (ulcer/cancer)*
02.05	*two ducklings*	*cat*
03.05	*one Nankeen night heron*	*?*
07.05	*4 scarlet ibises*	*?*
08.05	*one emu*	*botulism??*
10.05	*one white-cheeked macaw*	*cat*
10–11.05	*one scaly weaver*	*stolen?*
10.05	*pelican*	*pecked to death by marabou*
12.05	*one Bactrian camel*	*anaesthesia, hump procedure*
13.05	*one Senegal parrot*	*disappeared*
13–14.05	*tapir*	*stoning, vandalism*
16.05	*Rothschild's giraffe*	*autops.: cardiac jelly stress?*
20.05	*Somalian crocodile*	*bitten during fight*
23.05	*waterbuck*	*injured by rival († anaesthesia)*
26.05	*sun bear*	*pneumonia*
27.05	*sea lion*	*98 yrs? check water temp*
29.05	*reticulated python*	*cut in two by a partition*
02.06	*one Egyptian cobra*	*frozen alive (missing antidote)*
04.06	*Armenian mouflon*	*excoriation front paws (links?) † cervical rupture*

The press is tipped off and the national dailies quickly pick it up and run with it, they can smell a good story. The more zealous journalists uncover numerous other deaths, including that of a jharal, a Himalayan goat and also a New

Zealand tahr, without realising that these three names in fact refer to the same animal and it has already been included in the inventory. It hardly matters, since these days the role of journalism is first and foremost to prolong the reverberations of tragedy.

Petitions are signed and protests follow, there's a call for the new company to be brought to account. The authorities commit to multiple enquiries, some indeed are opened and one of them is even concluded: it makes the unambiguous finding that the abrupt change in management, staff and diets constituted a fatal blow to the zoo's residents. Councillor Fontanarosa publicly accuses Cosmo, who points the finger at minority shareholder Cressi, the young American director is sacked. It is not enough to reassure the public who are upset to learn that zoos aren't theme parks and that unlike Winnie-the-Pooh or Mickey, real animals are mortal. Out on the street, the brightly coloured posters fade, the smiling lion cubs are covered in graffiti.

The Zoological Society of London had abandoned its hope of providing a home to the last tamandin, and was consoling itself with the corpses of the second- and third-last specimens that had been entrusted to England's best taxidermist. Externally, their bodies were in perfect condition: the tamandins, armadillos and the okapi had been carried off by a lung infection preceded by encephalitis-induced seizures. Autopsies had examined things down to microscopic levels, biologists had triturated samples looking for a parasite, mycosis or a bacterium, but in vain. So the search had continued deeper still, at a cellular level, and there the culprit was hidden: its unofficial moniker was *the little bastard*, being the exclamation uttered by Doctor Nadia Monk the first time she noticed it under her microscope. She invited her assistants to come and observe the virus. It was quite pretty, it resembled Sardinia as seen from a satellite.

Tamandins had also been killed by a thogotovirus in the wild, a few scattered individuals that had been observed and counted for the last time in the 1960s near Kodok, on the northern border of what is now South Sudan. Nadia Monk wondered if the little thing she had under her eyes could have been responsible for the end of a species. It remained to be understood how the little bastard had managed to be introduced into the London Zoo, forty-odd years later and 5550 kilometres away. People postulated a Trojan horse theory, a capacity for latency: perhaps the virus had always been there, embedded deep within the creatures, waiting for the right moment to express itself. Requests were sent to every museum likely to have preserved the body of a tamandin, a hair even. It was the beginning of a laborious and specialised study, the kind of research that a BBC documentary would generously call *an enthralling zoological enquiry.*

In the years which follow the Roman slaughter, Parco Natura's partners frown at the sight of every new balance sheet. They had reckoned on one million ticket sales annually, but 2003 numbers are scarcely a third of that amount. The state is called in to the rescue, and of course the state comes rushing in. The public company is converted into a foundation, which facilitates its bailing out. Cosmo and Cressi each retain their seats on the board, but from now on they sit at the far end of the big table, somewhat in the shadows: they're waiting and watching. The municipality tries to get things back on an even keel, to smooth away the horrors of the past, a new director is appointed, as is, in March 2005, a certain Guido Anselmo Moro. After attending board meetings, Doctor Moro surmises the institution's days are numbered. He sees the business men already looking out the window, he knows that all it will take for the zoo to close its gates once and for all, is for Cosmo and Cressi to pull out.

But first of all, the gardens must be cleaned up, and this is where the new management directs its attention. Moro rids the zoo of all the paintwork that has been poisoning his residents, he undertakes minor renovations which will pass unnoticed by the public, because they're aimed at the animals' well-being. He dismisses the young, dynamic and underpaid employees, he recruits accredited keepers.

Thus it is that one fine morning in July of 2006, four years from retirement, Salvatore Leonardi dons his jacket once more and leaves his little lower-ground office in the museum. He pushes open the glass door to the terrace and, feeling emotional, somewhat hesitantly goes down the stone steps to the zoo. The locker rooms have been repainted but he chooses the same numbered locker as before. Management has made him responsible for an anteater, a cassowary and two pygmy hippopotamuses paddling about in their swampy marsh, in front of the eroding walls of the antiquated pachyderm house. The bas-reliefs look down on him silently: pharaohs and jackal-headed gods, half-hidden by the voracious ivy. He is unaware of what lies afoot in the mysterious workings of the powers that be, he has his feet in the mud, a bucket in his hand, he is happy. Once again he starts telling stories to passers-by, all the stories he has held in during these long years, the stories that have been tumbling around in his head or that he has murmured aloud to the stuffed animals. And sometimes his stories get tangled up, Salvatore rambles on a little and the visitors who recognise him hurry by when they spot him. One evening in the winter of 2009 he stops somebody new, a woman he thinks is beautiful, and who has just been appointed head of marketing and communications.

Giovanna and Moro had taken advantage of Oscar's relocation to revisit the entire flow chart of people moving around the zoo. In order to avoid visitors heading straight to the aviary and then leaving against the flow, they had to come up with a route that was circular, and mandatory. They would be made to go past the elephant house, they would then be sent along the southern boundary, past the lycaons, they would continue up the path to the macaques on their islet, then to the ex-penguinarium and the lake – they would cross the bridge, go past the museum, the bears, the dromedaries, take the underground walkway and then would only have to go up the steps to reach the tamandin. They would do a tour of the Great Aviary, in a clockwise direction, then be brought through the Reptilarium, and back out the zoo's second entrance, which would be re-opened.

Giovanna was sorry that visitors would no longer be able to wander wherever they pleased, which was after all the primary purpose of a zoological garden, all due respect to Moro. They'll still have a few options, the doctor conceded, a little freedom, to begin with. But this strategy will mean the gardens as a whole are able to benefit from the notoriety of this final specimen. And most importantly we'll avoid any crushing and jostling of crowds, he added, and Giovanna could not help but smile at the vanity of the comment.

Contrary to Moro's advice, she organised an internal information session: she didn't think the public could be convinced without the initial support of the more limited circle of employees. But the keepers turned the meeting into a chorus of complaints. These men who had always been so scornful of the public were now riven by jealousy: nobody was stopping in front of their animals anymore, they said, they were only interested in Leonardi's beast – and Leonardi, seated at the back of the room, remained as silent as his tamandin. Other complaints followed, the ticket-sellers needed more assistance and a raise, even the administration's concierge felt he was overworked. To hear him, you'd have thought he was the last bastion against hordes of homeless people and journalists, his waiting room was full and the sofa still hadn't been repaired, *la signora direttrice* was not unaware of the fact that two weeks earlier, there had been a vandalism incident, you should see it, somebody had torn one of the armrests, it was as though it had been bitten. A secretary mentioned a coffee machine that no longer returned change, the rumblings grew and Giovanna thought she heard somebody saying that if things continued like this, they would have to get rid of the creature. She thanked them all for coming and sent them on their way, *sotto voce,* straight to hell.

Her secretary informed her of a request from the London Zoo regarding a hair from the tamandin, she thought somebody was having her on: the day before, a local artist had begged her to preserve the animal's faeces, from which he was hoping to create an artwork. Giovanna rarely ventured out of the building now, for fear of inviting attention from some importunate person, she devoured salads in front of her screen and kept an eye on the entrance to the zoo from a first-floor window. The line of visitors. The scattered figures wandering around. Sometimes she did a round along the paths, after closing, but she only ever encountered the cleaning crews.

Dinners followed, one after the other, invitations she was unable to refuse because they involved important people, or old girlfriends who were suddenly insistent. They would then ask her if it really was something they should see, this tamandin that was the talk of the town, and Giovanna would start by shrugging her shoulders: there were indeed plenty of people who travelled thousands of kilometres to see a painting by Caravaggio, or one of Bernini's sculptures. Obviously, it was quite an opportunity for the zoo, to have custody of something that couldn't be seen anywhere else, something, soon enough, that nobody would ever be able to see again... For this beautiful creature's days were indeed numbered, Giovanna would murmur, adding in a confidential tone that she seriously expected to have to limit entries, and that it would be prudent to get in quickly. Giovanna was not lying, or not really – but depending on who she was talking to, she would replace her reference to works of art with the name of a local football celebrity or some other curiosity, the Pope or the Bocca della Verità. Because even to her closest friends, Giovanna would never give away the reasons she'd been hired – or perhaps it was more accurate to say it was a cruel fact that she lacked any real friends.

In the months prior to Giovanna's arrival, nobody would have bet on the zoo experiencing a renaissance. There was no vision, nor were there the funds to support any such vision, because the city had suffered the full blow of a global financial crisis. The parasitic interests lurking at the heart of the board had changed strategy: desperate to render the institution profitable, they had resolved to hasten its downfall.

You only had to look to the evidence, animals and business interests did not make good bedfellows, declared the shortest of them, refilling his glass. Especially whole animals, replied the taller of them, as they clinked glasses. The two men were sitting on a terrace overlooking Central Park, or perhaps they were somewhere else, they were the sort who travelled a lot. Distances, for them, were of little importance, they did, however, have a very strong feel for surface areas, and their potential yield. Seventeen hectares in the heart of Rome, now that was the sort of thing that would have politicians drooling, something they in turn could sell to voters as future municipal swimming pools, crèches or nursing homes. So these men were planning to redraw the zoo's boundaries, to nibble away at its edges, as they dreamt of dismembering the entire beast. And with the help of the champagne, they came up with even more ambitious projects, in the form of a riddle. What do the Romans most like to do on the weekend?

I suppose they do what everybody does, answered the shorter one, they go to the mall. Bingo, said the taller one, a twinkle in his eye. And the two men exchanged stories of their own retail experiences, Aviapark mall in Moscow, the Plaza in Jaipur and what was that gigantic pyramid called, the one in Malaysia? What they'd need is a plan, a model, so people can actually imagine it ... You're not serious? said one. Wanna bet? said the other – and chuckling madly, our fellows went through their contacts, made phone calls, calls which bounced from one corner of the globe to another, from Panama to Geneva, via Singapore, until they had snared the perfect architect. Discreet, invisible. An Algerian who was supposed to have designed a few attractive things in Dubai – not so much in the vertical-monumental style, more *outlet village*, you see, that would be ideal. And the two men fell silent, intoxicated by the magical vision conjured up by those words: an outlet village in the heart of Rome, or, more precisely, the model of an outlet village set down on the mayor's desk, because they had a nose for business, these men, as well as an appetite for the game.

And so, one evening in September 2009 a telephone rang, in the apartment of Chahine Gharbi. The man who was calling was perfectly sober, perhaps because he was calling from Riyadh, or perhaps because he was taking things a little too seriously. He was talking about a job, a project, something big, along the lines of what Chahine had done in Dubai but he couldn't say any more, it was all highly confidential. I understand, Chahine had replied, understanding nothing at all but nonetheless agreeing to go to Rome for further discussions. When he hung up, the silence in the apartment was heavier. They're saying it'll just be two weeks or so, said Chahine, and his words hung in the darkness for a long time. It's fine, a voice answered, finally. His wife appeared in the doorway to the living room. She had such dark shadows under her eyes that Chahine feared she might faint, and yet he did not move towards her, and she stood there, immobile, in the living room doorway. It's fine, the woman repeated. It's just what you need, a trip, a project.

The month of March arrived in a burst of radiance. At peak times all the ticket counters were operating, even on ordinary weekdays, and from up in her office, Giovanna noted with a wicked satisfaction that the ticket-sellers no longer had time to do their nails. She herself barely had a minute to bite her own: her secretary was constantly poking her head through the door to pass on a message, a sandwich or some candidate for a new assistant's position. None of them was appropriate, in any event Giovanna was in the sort of mood to refuse even the most sparkling CVs – her secretary was, moreover, reluctant to usher through the pair of graphic designers whom she feared she'd be scraping off the floor when it came time for them to leave.

Their new proposal clearly marked out the mandatory, circular route, and as soon as she saw it represented like that, one big, smooth, yellow loop, Giovanna regretted spoiling the space. It spelled the end of the garden and its meanderings, there would be no more harmless flirting in the bushes, no more surprises, no more coincidences or unexpected encounters. Looking at this new brochure, there was no choice but to be drawn to the Great Aviary. In this regard, the graphic artists had demonstrated some admirable creativity: the tamandin was represented by a cut-out shape, a hole in the paper. Giovanna traced her finger over the delicately carved-out little shape. The designers launched into a defence of their work but while they were speaking, Giovanna stood up, quietly skirted around them, as if not to disturb them, took her jacket off its hook and, as she closed the door behind her, gave them an embarrassed smile.

A smile that simply tried to say: don't be angry with me, it's stronger than I am, and indeed Giovanna could no longer bear it. Her heels clattered over the road that cut through the zoo, she turned a deaf ear to the line of vendors who had set themselves up there, all offering the same things for sale, tamandins as far as the eye could see, inflatable ones, plastic ones, fluffy ones, and their insistent cries combined with her own thoughts, which were trying to slow her steps. It was not as though she had signed any contract with the man, he had made her no promises, so why did she feel entitled to go looking for him, you're behaving like a schoolkid, old girl, she thought as she went up the front steps of the Hôtel des Princes.

She recognised one of the receptionists and, alas, it was reciprocated: she saw it in his eyes. How awkward it is, to encounter by day, humans one has only previously encountered by night. But he greeted her in English, imagining her perhaps to be foreign, or out of tact. She did not disabuse him of the notion, but she muddled her words as she asked to see *Mister Gharbi*, all the while anxious to know if he might have left a message, a message for her – and instantly regretting the question, which then required her to provide her name. The receptionist did not let her dig herself any deeper into the hole. He raised his powerless hands: it had been ten days since *the gentleman* had shown any sign of life, and nobody knew how to contact him. She raised her eyes enquiringly towards the upper floors, but the man explained to her that they'd had to vacate the room. There's a lot of demand, you know, because of what's happening at the zoo – and he pointed to a sign behind Giovanna: the hotel was hosting a conference on the tamandin, which explained the hubbub in the foyer, where attendees were gathering to resounding greetings of *caro collega* or *illustre professore*, clapping each other heartily on the back.

The receptionist hesitated, looking at the woman intently. Then he bent down to pick something up, a black briefcase, which he put on the counter. This was all *Mister Gharbi* had left behind, in the room. But there was also, he added, clearing his throat and tapping away on his keyboard ... A message? No, said the man, an invoice – and he printed a long strip of white paper which he delicately set down on the briefcase, and Giovanna understood that these two items were inseparable. The amount at the foot of the page was all the more astonishing for the fact it referred only to items from the minibar: the sum of an interminable procession of beers, peanuts and chocolate bars, plus a small bottle of prosecco, which stood out. The room itself had been paid for by his employer, the receptionist confided. But they were not responsible for the extras. They hadn't heard anything from him either, but between you and me, he added in a murmur, suddenly switching into Italian, *credo che se ne fregano,* I don't think they give a damn, frankly. Giovanna leaned in a little towards the man and, lowering her voice, said: Have you opened it? *La valigetta*? The receptionist shook his head and, keeping one eye on his colleague, gently opened the lid. The bag was empty, apart from a small brochure. An ad, in Arabic, spruiking the features of a shopping centre: a renovated souk, old stone buildings, a fountain-filled square, passers-by in djellabahs, laden with paper shopping bags, and printed on the last page an array of well-known brands. She put it back where it came from and closed the briefcase once more. Visibly sorry, the receptionist shrugged his shoulders, Giovanna sighed and pointed to the bill. Will the hotel file a complaint, for the invoice? The man answered yes, unfortunately, that was the procedure for outstanding bills.

So Giovanna took out her credit card and handed it to the man. And with that simple, calculated gesture, she erased everything: the chocolate bars, the peanuts, the beers, and the little bottle of prosecco too. She relegated it all to the oblivion of settled accounts. The receptionist provided her with a receipt which she crumpled up, already casting about for a rubbish bin, an ashtray where she might abandon this scrap of a souvenir. As for the briefcase, the hotel could either keep it, or offer it to one of the symposium members. People held conferences for an animal that was about to disappear, but she was not about to organise a seminar around some guy who'd done a runner. That particular species was some way from going extinct, she thought, pushing the revolving door. Standing on the steps outside, Giovanna was overwhelmed by a suffocating sadness.

While Giovanna was drowning her bitterness in her work, the public was going wild for the last tamandin. Zoologists debated the origin of its scaly spine or discussed its level of intelligence, which they suspected to be extremely high. The animal had revived the paleontologists' dispute over the grouping of placental mammals – even though it was a cousin of the aardvark, according to the medullary structure of its teeth, its similarity to *Myrmecophaga tridactyla* pointed towards the hypothetical Atlantogenata clade. Others considered it a taxon stemming from the Laurasiatheria, straddling the Pholidota and Perissodactyla – that's to say, in fact straddling a horse. And some classified it exclusively in that last taxonomic rank, together with rhinoceroses and tapirs, given its number of claws: they saw it as a direct descendent of the mythical African chalicothere, which cast a new light on the legend of the Nandi bear, said to suck out the brains of sheep, and which one could not help but compare with the fabled Japanese *baku*, said to suck up children's nightmares with its trunk.

The most serious-minded of the scientists shrugged, the species had already been the subject of ample studies and they knew exactly what they were dealing with. The recent genealogy of tamandins had been documented, its genealogical tree used to span several countries, it started to thin out with increased interzoo exchanges, and single or difficult births, and its frail branches all finished up with a cross. The first Roman tamandin had arrived from Genoa in 1943, following the bombing of that city: Oscar's great-great-great-grandmother. He himself was born in December 1987, in a zoo in its death throes, earning only a brief mention in a register that was promptly misplaced. The absence of a birth certificate was enough to feed implausible rumours, people imagined a breed sullied by some unorthodox cross-fertilisation.

But only the most extravagant of discoveries deserved an airing before the general public. Giovanna came across the account of a young man from Milan alleged to have entered the aviary, by night, and to have been attacked by the creature. It was said to have knocked him to the ground, followed by an attempt to suck out his brains: the young man approached the camera to show off his pierced ear drum, and the brown-crusted ear did the rounds of the social networks, accompanied by the image of a brain scan and commentary from a man in a white coat who confirmed that the adolescent had lost part of his encephalon. Giovanna showed the absurd video to Moro, who did not for a second doubt that the adolescent was suffering from a serious lack of grey matter. But what Giovanna wished to draw to his attention was the figure below the image indicating the number of views. For the first time, she had the pleasure of seeing dawn on the doctor's face an expression of absolute and utter astonishment.

It was in mid-March that the elephant house and penguinarium were reconfigured. The former was only partially occupied, and its main room was dedicated to an educational exhibit where the public was able to familiarise itself with the habits of the tamandin. One section was dedicated to its diet, where one could read that tamandins do not feed on brains but rather on fruit and insects, and in particular, ants, in the order of several tens of thousands a day. A large screen displayed the zoo's efforts to meet the needs of its exceptional guest: a lurching little van climbed up a forest path, an anthill was gathered up by the shovel-load, keepers dug a hole under the Great Aviary's beech tree, into which they tipped twigs, insects and larvae – and the images went round on loop. The other walls were covered with illustrations and text devoted to the anatomy of the tamandin or to its lifestyle and habits. There one learned they had been very solitary creatures, who had only spent time in the company of their own kind during reproductive periods. In order to find a partner, tamandins had not utilised a vocal call, but rather had tracked their fellow creatures in silence, following the olfactory traces they had left in their wake. It was Moro who insisted that all verbs relating to the animal's social existence be expressed in the past tense.

The exhibit was all temporary, of course, and was installed over just a few days. Some visitors commented on the sweltering heat, the persistent bluebottle flies, and also the smell. From time to time, terrible trumpeting sounds could be heard behind the plasterboard panels that had been hastily thrown together.

That evening, Giovanna told her husband about the chaotic installation of the exhibit, a subject of really only marginal interest to him, and also how she had met Salman Rushdie, which had him suddenly raising his head. It was the director who had announced that he was coming. The author was spending a few days in Rome, he wanted to visit the zoo and see the tamandin. She had heard of Rushdie, although his name meant nothing more to her than a little incendiary notoriety, but Moro had been in rhapsodies over the visit and had impressed upon her its significance. They had planned to offer the author a complete tour of the institution and its new installations, perhaps taking in the Zoological Museum, and the director had contacted a caterer and had a generous buffet prepared in the conference room, should it be required.

The following day, a car had set down a short, plump, weary-looking man outside the gates. Giovanna hadn't really known what to expect, she was simply relieved to understand almost everything he said, his diction was slow and clear, his manners courteous, he had politely refused the program she had planned, he just wanted to see the tamandin. Giovanna had accompanied him into the aviary, to the great irritation of those gathered at the gates. The author had then stopped to exchange a few words with Moro, and half an hour later had departed again.

Her husband plied her with questions, demanding details. She was surprised at the pride she felt at having awoken his curiosity. That night, they made love.

It was the following day that she found the coat. Or rather, it was the tradesmen who discovered it, in the penguinarium they were renovating. It was hanging from a doorknob, a long, dirty, grey coat one might well have tossed in the bin, or left at the ticket desks, where lost and found items were piled in a heap, but in the coat was a passport and they thought it better to hand it over to management. The coat remained hanging in Giovanna's office all morning, next to her own jacket. And all morning, Giovanna worked, which is to say, she spoke on the telephone, she stared at a computer screen, every now and again she clicked on a link. And the whole time, she didn't once look at the grey coat, for the presence of the coat masked everything else.

It was only when lunch time came around that she found the strength to empty its pockets, carefully. She started by pulling out a phone charger and its tangled cord, and then some chocolate bar wrappers. Five, six copies of old zoo brochures. More chocolate bar wrappers. And the passport, dog-eared and Algerian, which she slipped into her jacket before leaving.

In the penguinarium, there was much hammering and sweeping, dust glittered in the light. The foreman continued to munch on his sandwich as he answered Giovanna: no, they had found nothing else, old blankets, beer cans, what was she expecting, spider webs, cigarette stubs, the usual things you're likely to find in an abandoned space. But as she could see it was clean now, look, they were almost finished replacing the windows, tomorrow they'd be painting, two coats of the black would be enough, I'm not making any promises but everything should be ready by Friday. That is, if we're allowed to get on with our work, the man added, muttering, because Giovanna had started inspecting the nooks and crannies, shifting tool boxes and planks with her foot, getting in the way of the tradesmen, searching in vain for something that may have been overlooked, tracks, a trace.

Since its unfortunate conception in the 1960s, the penguinarium had primarily served as a storage area. It had required the last specimen, and Moro and Giovanna's inventiveness, to reopen its doors. Ideally situated halfway along the loop, the penguinarium now offered the public the opportunity to have their first encounter with the peculiar creature. It was not a matter of providing further information about the species but rather of offering a first glimpse of the individual, showcasing a different angle of Oscar, a night-time angle, to be precise.

For the tamandin, so it was said, was an essentially nocturnal mammal: the creature had thus been filmed under infra-red light, so the images could then be projected on to the penguinarium's largest wall. The recording was presented unedited, and the experience felt like a contemporary art installation – it was a small space and the general public could not get any distance, they didn't really understand what they were seeing, what was being projected onto the wall, above their heads. There were flashes of a large white, longish mass, quivering foliage, what might have been a branch would suddenly disappear, before spectators were dazzled by the appearance of two moving headlights, for in the infrared glow the anteater's eyes shone like two suns. Most of the time, there was nothing to see, apart from the ground and the swarming ghost-like spectres of ants. The sound was as deafening as the image was outsized and the little building was filled with rustlings and rootings about, and distant cries – sometimes the regular whistle of breathing hushed the chattering of the visitors passing through, disoriented, at the bottom of the screen.

One thousand eight hundred kilometres to the north, deep within the London Zoo, veterinarian Nadia Monk was contemplating an image which to her seemed enormous, being only a few millimetres from her retina. She had discovered how the virus had been introduced into the zoo, she had the sinister vehicle under her very eyes: a tick, swollen and fat with blood. It made her shudder each time she saw its whole body, as she brought it into focus with the turn of a knob.

Ever since she was very young, Nadia Monk had loathed arachnids, paguroids, crabs, anything that even remotely resembled a spider – and she particularly abhorred acarids, which she was forced into contact with all too often by virtue of her job. There were tens of thousands of species, they were everywhere, and the largest of them, the ones which truly disgusted her, were the ticks. Ticks had the treacherous ability to remain inactive for years, a blind, deaf, withdrawn creature able to perfectly mimic death – and then it required almost nothing, just a little butyric acid, for it to start wriggling its feet, for it to attach itself to some passing animal, for it to slip into the forest of its fur and find an appropriate spot, some soft skin, into which it would plunge its rostrum and start sucking up blood – and at the same time start to spread all the filthy infectious bugs it was carrying into the host organism. Vicious little cunt, murmured Monk. Its actual name was *Amblyomma improbum*, it was the taxidermist who had discovered it, hidden between the scaly plates of Sheryl the tamandin. Where it was nice and warm between the scales, where the skin is most tender.

On opening it up to analyse the blood in its abdomen, she had noticed something unusual, rolled around one of the insect's legs. It was a filament, or rather, if considered from the creature's scale, a cumbersome bracelet it had been unable to shake off, twisted around the coxa, at the end of the trochanter. The microscope revealed a scaly stalk, a protein fibre which did not come from the tamandin: Monk was looking at a hair fibre from the subfamily Caprinae, and more specifically, a hair from *Ovis aries*. Its morphology and its diameter – imagine, barely 13 μm – left little room for doubt as to its origin. It was, as those humans less knowledgeable than Monk would call it, wool – and more precisely, to use the specific vocabulary of pullover manufacturers, merino wool.

Salman Rushdie's article appeared at the start of spring and in *The New York Times*, because he was a famous author and because he had managed, in a few well-honed phrases, to capture a sentiment of uniqueness, of ultimate solitude. First he sketched a portrait of Rome, this ancient, buried iceberg of a town, he retraced the steps of his visit to the Mithraeum, far beneath the Basilica of San Clemente, his contemplation of Bernini's immortal sculptures at the Villa Borghese, and then he came to his unexpected encounter with a creature of flesh and blood, a thing with neither past nor future, to which the major media outlets had as yet devoted little space. He compared the tamandin to some fantastical animal, he evoked griffins and dragons, he harkened back to the vanished unicorn. He then described the real creature in whose presence he found himself, the acrid odour of its enclosure, the bushes, the retreating animal, its little eyes with their swollen lids. Thirty million years had been distilled into this, had led to the shape of this claw, to the precise colour of those scales, to this perfect creation, as perfect as any of the rough drafts Nature is constantly producing – perfect and yet so vulnerable, so ill-adapted to the world. He mentioned the possibility of cloning, which would render the animal nothing more than a vulgar copy. What amounted to evolution, the author wrote, what might explain a line of descent, was less the replication of genes than the error which slipped into each generation, the little unexpected variable, the random encounters, the music of chance: now this was the stuff of life, and this, along with the tamandin, was what was going to disappear. In his view, the people were not mistaken. What they were there to see at the Rome Zoo was neither a collection of genes, nor even the condemned image of a race – it was a heartbeat, a being whose slow breathing, behind the thickets, was unique. Its tragic futility had rendered it an anomaly, a moment hanging from the thread of time, something swinging, like Schrödinger's cat, between monster and miracle. And the author wondered if Oscar was truly unaware of the extent of his remarkable condition. Or if the tamandin was indeed able, in one way or another, *to feel* that he was alone in the world.

Rushdie's article unleashed a lengthy series of reactions. Some readers shared their own emotion, others were irritated by the overly abstruse nature of the piece, some scientists had a good snigger, a few literary critics deplored his uncharacteristic lack of humour. People started talking about the tamandin in the most refined circles, those who closely follow the circles of power.

Most species are extinguished in silence, far from the eyes of onlookers and commentators. Take the golden toad of Monteverde, discovered by an explorer in 1964: a thousand yellow batrachians crawling around on an isolated rocky outcrop, deep in the Costa Rican jungle. In 1989, eleven examples of the species were counted, and a subsequent expedition found none. Similarly, take the ō'ō'ā'ā of Kauai, which left behind only a peculiar name and a short sound recording, made in 1987. Numerous ornithologists then searched the forests of Hawaii, pointing their mikes towards the tops of the tallest trees, but the call of the little passerine bird was never heard again. In contrast, several dodo bones were discovered, and several photos taken of the last quagga. More was known about the last thylacine because that unusual striped dog was filmed for seventy-two seconds in 1933, so there it is, moving around on the internet in black and white. It, too, became extinct far from global scrutiny, down in the bottom-right-hand section of Eurocentric planispheres, in Hobart, Tasmania, in a corner of its cage.

All of these animals had died too far removed from the gaze of onlookers, or too soon, thought Moro, as he wandered through the silent halls of the Zoological Museum, past the skeletons of pachyderms and orangutans. Reports of their extinction were merely items for inclusion in the scientific news in brief, they were relegated to the cellars of knowledge, no different to these growling, immobile creatures, behind their panes of glass. There was Fritz the bear, one paw in the air, his gaze blank, nobody aware of the fact that his was also a story of war. The skeleton of Mwana the elephant. And a mandrill that had just been stuffed, its face a mask fixed in a silent scream. None of these deaths had had time to make any sense, because nobody had been present to witness the final breaths.

Moro opened the French doors and the noise swelled as he went out to the terrace. He thanked old man Hagenbeck for having thought to design this viewing point, back in 1911, along with the spectacular view to the gardens, for it afforded him now a breathtakingly beautiful sight: there at his feet, along the long path that hugged the lake, a human river was coursing past on its way to see the last tamandin.

After visiting the exhibition and viewing the film at the penguinarium, visitors would finally climb the steps leading to the Great Aviary. There, high up, against a background of blue sky and metallic interlacing, a little male tui was performing his nuptial ballet of tailspins and nosedives. The bird landed on a branch of the black beech tree, he spread his wings, he puffed his feathers, gleaming colourfully in the sun, he tossed back his beak to show off his downy white neck – and the female tui watched him out of the corner of her eye, head tilted to one side, all ears as she listened to his amorous modulations.

But nobody was paying them any attention. Nobody admired the comings and goings of the three pukekos with their long, spider-like feet, jealously watching over the family eggs. Nobody commented on the curious beak of the African spoonbills, rummaging around in the reeds looking for twigs for their nest. Having made it thus far, the visitors fell quiet. One could barely make out the rustling of fabric, the scraping of the crowd's countless footsteps, as people quietly made their way around the aviary, their gaze riveted inwards. Every face was drawn towards the last tamandin – or more precisely, everybody was staring at the bush where it was sheltering, peering into the shadows of the small, blossoming myrtle, borne by the hope of a glimpse. The squawking of birds formed a backdrop to the silence.

Rare were the visitors lucky enough to catch sight of the tip of its snout, and rarer still those who had glimpsed all of it. People knew the tamandin led a secluded life and that this was its most precious entitlement – indeed, since the 1960s, this had been the right of every inhabitant of any self-respecting zoo. For an ability to conceal oneself was probably the closest thing to freedom – it was what animals spent most of their time doing, in their natural environment. Nobody would have dared deprive the last specimen of this right to be reticent, this final wish.

It was his mere presence people were seeking, even though some visitors still brandished their telephones, hoping to capture some movement, a leaf which may suddenly have quivered as the little animal went by. People knew he was dozing there, behind the shrubbery. Maybe he was watching the water glitter in the pond with his night-owl eyes, he could probably make out the birds that came to drink from it. But Oscar never ventured so far. When he did chance a few steps out into the open, a shiver ran through the crowd, a wave of hastily stifled murmurs. People jostled forwards even more, trying to catch a glimpse of its little head, its eyes blinking in the sunlight. He lifted his astounding snout, sniffing the air which was heavy with human scents. Sometimes he would arch his spine, and then start calmly, obstinately, scratching the earth. He didn't dig, as he would at night on the lookout for ants – in the daylight, he was happy just to scrape the dust with the back of his enormous claws, as if he were stroking the earth. Nobody, not even Moro, knew how to explain this behaviour. At the slightest noise, the animal would quickly retreat to the shade, like a hermit crab disappearing into its shell.

The Great Aviary was set over formwork which incorporated a half-buried shelter, hidden by vegetation from the public's sight. It's where tools were kept, it is where Salvatore spent his days. Small horizontal windows, lined up like arrow slits, allowed the keeper to monitor the whole aviary as well as the public as they slowly made their way along the fence, encircling him, so many eyes trained on him or almost on him, at the bushes flanking the shelter, only a few metres away.

The keeper no longer told stories to the visitors; there were far too many of them. There he stayed, in the shadows, hidden at the heart of all this attention, as if in the eye of a cyclone. In amongst the shovels, the pickaxes and hoses, he had installed shelving where he kept books and newspapers. Four times a day, a portable stove brought a blackened coffee maker to a rumbling gurgle. A mattress was rolled up in a corner. His lips moved in silence, in the darkness of the shelter. He would mumble things to the tamandin lying just a few metres from him, on the other side of a metal door with a small window. The door opened on to a broad cement threshold, protected by a straw awning. This is where the tamandin sheltered during stormy weather, or when it was very hot. When the old animal was lying there, right up against the door, Salvatore would listen to the whistle of its breath.

He, for one, understood what the little creature was doing, when it ventured out into the sun. In those moments, the tamandin was stroking its shadow.

By the end of March, the zoo was experiencing a degree of success that outstripped its capacity. There was no choice but to reinforce the balustrades along the pathway, it was clear that something which might perfectly well resist the force of a single individual became utterly useless in the face of the masses. The tarmac on the paths was cracking under the weight of countless footsteps. Benches were discovered broken in two, their slats snapped like matchsticks. A lamp post was found lying on the ground, disconcerting cracks were spotted in the walls of the penguinarium. The wooden bridge spanning the lake had to be condemned. Every evening, it was as if the gardens had been gnawed away, flattened by some gigantic, blind earthworm.

And added to the requirements of the other animals came the needs of this monster. To the containers of grain, fruit and meat which arrived every morning was now added the enormous delivery of foodstuffs intended for human consumption – thousands of sandwiches, bottles of water, chocolate bars, and ready-to-eat meals that ran out well before noon. More impressive still was the volume of out-flowing product: every day there was enough animal manure to almost fill a truck, and triple this volume was required to clear the human excretions. Portable toilets were now lined up in various places along the circuit, and come nightfall, battalions of street cleaners would sweep through the paths. All manner of items were discovered after closing time, shoes, backpacks, cameras as well as countless copies of zoo brochures which they very quickly stopped bothering to print.

A security firm was tasked with monitoring the external perimeter and with policing the area surrounding the gardens. Cameras were installed. But it was not a lack of physical security that was threatening the zoo: it was a lack of certainty. Significant investments ought to have been made in order to manage the general public and to safeguard the other animals. The tigers and monkeys were manifesting alarming signs of stress, they cowered, trembling, right at the back of their enclosures – their viewing windows were covered with black paint, in order to protect them from the unrest. The fragile life expectancy of the tamandin prevented any long-term strategising whatsoever, there was a sense of tinkering with provisional arrangements, of making do. Giovanna's secretary worried about her boss's health on seeing her face, hollowed out by the dark shadows under her eyes.

Knocks rang out at the door to the shelter. Every time, the old keeper would start before getting up to open it. Usually it was one of the *dottore*'s assistants, there to enquire after Oscar's health, but Salvatore always worried they were coming to tell him he no longer had a job. He had reached retirement age and any day now, it was inevitable, they would come to tell him it was over, that he could go home. His anxiety grew, it fed off his solitude and the emptiness of his hours, it merged with the darkness of the shelter and the shadows grew ever denser as they crawled towards him. That morning, the keeper felt truly afraid when he saw the silhouette of the *signora direttrice* outlined against the blinding sunlight.

She started by asking him the most banal of questions, she pretended to take a quick look at the animal, through the window in the door. But she had not come to talk to him about Oscar, nor even, as he feared, about his work. She had come for something else, something so removed from his own preoccupations that he struggled, initially, to understand what it was about. She spoke to him about a man, a man with a coat. Did he remember him, a man who had come to the zoo on a daily basis? Salvatore frowned, staring at the passport she was showing him. He used to come often, she insisted, he used to come every day, sometimes I would be with him, Giovanna repeated.

Salvatore was remembering, yes. The fellow who used to look a little stooped when he walked. Yes, of course, in fact he remembered him very well. To begin with, the man used to come alone, they had often stopped for a chat, although I was always the one doing the talking, Salvatore clarified, he would listen, he would ask questions about the zoo, its architecture, how the animals lived. It's unusual, normally people come and walk past and then go again but he used to have time, he did, he used to come often, you're right, he used to come often and sometimes with you, too, a coat, yes. But that was in winter, it was before the whole business with Oscar, when nobody was around. No, I haven't seen him since, you know, with all these people now ... No, I never understood why he came, I couldn't tell you. To begin with I thought he was mad. You know, there are a lot of people who come on their own, I've seen so many of them, if you want to sit down, I have another chair over there, I can tell you, I've seen some bizarre people. There was one fellow, it was a few years ago now, a fellow who used to come in the evenings, he'd stand outside the cages and he'd, I'm sorry, I probably shouldn't tell you this, he'd do things in front of the animals, we had to chase him off but sometimes he would come back at night, after closing. They ended up arresting him, the police. Most of the time they're inoffensive, sometimes though it gets ugly. You're too young, you wouldn't have heard about Nicoletta, it was in 1980, or 1981? Everybody recognised her because she truly was *una bella ragazza*, if you don't mind my saying so, just imagine, she had fallen in love with Shere Khan, you wouldn't have known him either, it wasn't that he was wicked, he used to recognise her because she'd come to visit several times a week. She'd talk to him, she would give him things. One day, it was in autumn, he was lying right up close to the bars and she had climbed up on the railing, she'd slipped her hand between the bars, to stroke him and the keeper … back then it was Maurizio who was looking after the big cats, Maurizio or Enzo? I don't know anymore, I think it was Maurizio … he tried to warn the girl, but it was already too late, the tiger had ripped off her whole arm, right up to here, up to her shoulder. It's just that, you know, animals don't all have the same way of showing their affection … But people come, they pass through, they don't listen … I'm going to tell you something, it's something I've worked out over the years, I shouldn't … but people who go to zoos all the time, there's always something the matter with them. Unless, Salvatore went on to clarify, they have children.

Outside the Great Aviary, even parents were quiet. Quite possibly, they were unable to find the right words, quite possibly, they didn't know how to tell this particular story, or what happy moral to the tale might be extracted from it. In any event there were very few families, now. The zoo had been invaded by crowds but it had been deserted by children. And Giovanna shivered, as she looked out at the public from the keeper's underground shelter. Old Leonardi was right. Zoological gardens used to belong to the world of childhood, she and Moro had violated sacred territory. They had brought hordes of adults into a protected playing field, a sanctuary of innocence. And they would be made to pay for it. She did not know how, but Giovanna suddenly sensed that all this could only end badly. She imagined swarms of bloodthirsty locusts, storms of biblical proportions, these things only ever happened in books, but that was not enough to reassure her. After all, the ground could well open up beneath their feet. These crowds, whom she herself had summoned, made her nauseous. And with each new visitor, the memory of the foreigner grew a little dimmer; in a place repeatedly trampled under the weight of so many millions of footsteps, his tracks were disappearing.

She realised the old keeper was still rambling on, next to her. That this deluge of words, the teeming torrent of his memories, just kept pouring out, with little regard to her. He too could go to hell, with his memory in tatters. He had forgotten that Chahine didn't speak a word of Italian, he had dreamed up impossible conversations. How could he have helped her, this poor man mouldering away in the shadows of his shelter, feeling his way through the fog of his memories. It was him. He was the first one, the first victim of this creature with the protruding snout and the little yellow eyes, the tamandin. And only now did it dawn on her how grotesque she truly thought it was.

Visitors were coming now from afar to see the creature, and the popularity of the zoo was not without its consequences. People were starting to worry, in the offices of the Capitoline Assembly. Obscure parishes had lodged complaints, conveyed by the bishops to the Vatican itself: pilgrims were suffering, Italian transport companies were overwhelmed and there was a lack of hotel accommodation, trips had been cancelled. The city of Rome is bloated with government departments, bursting with thousand-year-old monuments, and it is also home to a Pope, meaning there is already quite a lot to manage: the public transport system had always struggled to beat a path through the tourist crowds. This added attraction was threatening to paralyse it.

Things were particularly problematic in the immediate surrounds of the Villa Borghese, an area where embassies rub shoulders with banks and affluent residences, a privileged neighbourhood ill-accustomed to crowds. Locals complained of the sudden noise, the traffic, the clamour of vendors, the double-parked triple-decker buses. The mayor, Alemanno, was annoyed, because the area constituted an influential section of his electorate – it really did take the cake, that something no bigger than a dog could bring entire neighbourhoods to a standstill. His fellow councillors whispered ideas into his ears that only served to irritate him further, yes of course you could install new traffic lights, implement one-way systems, build elevated walkways, broaden the Via del Corso, of course! You could even bring in experts from Mecca while you're at it, and draw up spiral-shaped plans! But who is going to pay for it? Will you? The anteater?

Calls were made to the zoo in order to find out how long this circus was going to carry on, and the director raised his arms heavenwards for, really, God only knew.

In London, Nadia Monk's eyes were weary from looking at a screen and scrolling through security camera video footage in the zoo's surveillance control room. A single camera covered the area of interest to her, the one that had been affected by the lightning-swift epizootic: it showed an angle from the okapi's enclosure, and the viewing terrace overlooking the tamandin's section. Nadia held down the fast-forward button, shapes flitted backwards and forwards on the screen like flies in a jar, every now and again one or other of them froze, or frantically waved their arms about before blending back in with the thrumming crowd of visitors, their leaping children and their speedy strollers. The shadows grew noticeably longer, sometimes an animal made a mad dash back into the tall grasses. It was all very tiring for the biologist, who was used to the indolent life that normally stretched out beneath the lens of her microscope – and it was more testing still for the security supervisor pacing back and forth behind her, struggling to hide his impatience. It was now precisely eleven nights that she had been occupying his chair.

As there is nothing of particular interest to see on the screen, we can spend some time describing the security officer's routine. Every evening, after organising his colleagues' rounds, John White was in the habit of settling down in his chair to indulge his secret passion, a passion contained entirely in the books and reviews he kept hidden in the bottom drawer of his desk. John had a weakness: he was a poet. And, another matter of which he was even more guilty: he read poetry. Truth be told, he had a soft spot for W.H. Auden and the New Mexican School. He had made his way through several casual, poorly paid positions before landing the job of *Chief Security Officer, nights, ZSL*, which perfectly suited his predilection for the silence of words. And it better explains his irritation at having to deal with the small woman who had been sitting in his chair until the wee hours for over a week now. John did not agree with Nadia Monk's absurd hypothesis, this allegedly wilful introduction of a virus. It was like something out of a crime novel, a literary genre for which John reserved a particular distaste. Nadia's persistence relied on some vague notions about incubation periods, acarids and merino wool filaments, she simply couldn't come around to the idea of the anteaters' accidental death – she was firmly of the opinion that some deliberate human intervention had upended the laws of nature, along with the laws of plausibility. So, while the vet felt she was trying to find logical, reasoned grounds for there being one remaining specimen, in John's view, she had in fact succumbed to some dangerous whim of an idea.

He thus made an ill-concealed show of disbelief as Nadia tried to demonstrate her findings, after letting out the crudest of curses as she feverishly tried to find the pause button. She brought her face close to the screen so she could better make out the quivering shape, in the grainy image, and John joined her in the glow of the monitor. He saw nothing out of the ordinary on the little viewing platform. The long shadows of a sunny morning. A man's back, a coat, an umbrella and a grey hat, arm raised. Nadia rewound a few seconds, to show him the whole sequence: the man in the coat approaching the railing, his arm directed towards the sky. John shrugged, Nadia was insistent, look closer. Look at him, at the man in the heavy coat, as he approaches, as he leans right up against the railing. At his hand emerging from his pocket, as it disappears to gather momentum, only to suddenly lift, his arm sweeping through space in a generous arc – and it is then that John recognises the action:

The dusk approaches, spreads its wing,
As, with the day, life's rumours fade;
Now reaching stars the sower's shade
Enhances every patient fling.

But John did not recite the lines aloud. He contented himself with mumbling, to the veterinarian's great disappointment, that he couldn't make out anything except yet another person throwing peanuts.

Doctor Moro was admiring the screen of his new telephone, slumped in one of the green rooms at the RAI television studios. It was complicating the work of the make-up artist leaning over him, who was trying as best she could to powder his cheeks. If power does curious things to people's faces, fame, too, works its own minor effects: as a general rule, it lightens the complexion. But the ethologist was too absorbed to make note of that.

The popularity of the last specimen had surpassed his every expectation, marching into territories that the doctor had, until then, overlooked. He was discovering a limitless continent, held in the palm of his hand. Alerts notified him whenever the word *tamandin* so much as showed its snout – and since the animal was holding court atop every search engine list, his telephone never stopped vibrating. The internet was crawling with shots snatched of the Rome Zoo, to which were added the most ludicrous photomontages. The tamandin on the moon. The tamandin in a Yoda outfit. The tamandin sitting behind the desk in the Oval Office, the tamandin scampering along the Great Wall, the tamandin in my bathroom. And the deeper Moro dug, the more insight the anteater offered him into forms of wildlife whose existence he had never so much as suspected. DIY fanatics, demonstrating how to make your own tamandin costume for a night of S&M. Discerning food lovers creating recipes based on a type of never-before-tasted flesh. And hordes of millenarian neo-punks for whom Oscar was, quite simply, the symbol of the end of time.

The scientist was called upon to lead publications, chair colloquiums, he was invited onto programs dedicated to the solitary creature, to animal conservation or to the Anthropocene, none of it interested him as much as the digital manifestation of his success – and as the studio's make-up artist did her best to tame his bushy eyebrows, behind the glasses he refused to remove, Moro discovered that little gesture peculiar to our new humanity: the slide of a thumb from right to left across the smooth surface of a screen, to watch at ever-increasing speed the passing images of our aimless wanderings.

Coming home late one night in April, Giovanna accidentally dropped an Algerian passport onto the doormat as she was looking for her keys. Her husband didn't ask any questions as he picked it up, Giovanna nonetheless made some excuse, as pointless as it was inaudible. The fact was, she was surprised herself to rediscover the item in her handbag.

In the moments when she found herself alone, Giovanna had often leafed through the little book, tracing her fingers over the coat of arms, over the interwoven geometric lines that covered the pages. She had brushed over the perforations, the little iridescent disc, the miniscule embossed inscriptions, all of which rendered the document unique and impossible to forge. Notwithstanding the fact that the words had been translated into French, the sinuous scrolls of its national language remained as mysterious as Chahine himself, and to Giovanna, the alphabet described the breath of an evening breeze, or the ephemeral tracing of a fingernail on the back of a neck. The personal details were of no interest to her, and she had never stopped to linger over the photograph, over the rigid, cadaver-like face. Stroking the paper's surface, her fingers sought only to revive her own memories, of the features, the scent, the sound of a voice from an affair she was gradually forgetting.

Sometimes she still thought she caught his profile, in a crowd, or the line of a shoulder that could only have been his.

In the time it took to open the window, the mirage had disappeared, swallowed up in the stream of bodies. Her imaginings had become increasingly rare, and the passport had slowly slipped towards a corner of her desk, pushed aside by letters and contracts and files.

In contrast, however, her own career had forged ahead in leaps and bounds. She could now return favours, offer exclusives. Her name was bandied about in influential circles, she fell out of touch with numerous contacts only to acquire those more powerful. But if success had fleshed out her wardrobe, it did not make her more radiant. Giovanna slept the sleep of the dead, she no longer dreamt, yet every morning she woke up feeling numb to the bone, weighed down by an endless exhaustion. And her husband kept telling her she must take a break, if she wasn't feeling well – all the while insisting on taking her out to dinners only he was interested in. There she would describe, for the umpteenth time, the beauty of the scales, the subtle shading of its hair, the animal's touching timidity and the funny way it would, all of a sudden, snuffle up thousands of crawling ants. Nobody could imagine what it was thinking, or the way in which it conceived the world – but one thing was certain, Giovanna would conclude in a voice betraying the hint of a tremor, that on its death, it was our entire universe that would, as a result, be diminished.

Not everybody was swayed by Giovanna's assertions: there were sceptics, those who are on principle wary of fads. They wondered what on earth could be attracting the masses in this way, they discussed the matter amongst themselves, in the end, they just wanted to confirm the phenomenon with their own eyes, and most of them kept going back to the zoo as often as they could.

One group of students from La Sapienza University tried to implement an ongoing research project, under the auspices of their sociology degree. They prepared a ten-page questionnaire to which random visitors replied, in the scramble at the entrance and the melee at the exit. The research group succeeded only in ascertaining that every socio-cultural milieu had been affected, that there was a marginally greater number of men who visited, but that this differential was not conclusive given the margins for error. Further studies which were better structured failed to offer better results: there was nothing to do but leave it to the philosophers to expound on the subject.

These latter jostled with one another to impose their own interpretation on events, they considered the tamandin to be a sign of a return to paganism, an allegory of singularity, a metaphor for the end of Europe or the incarnation of a new ontological realism, amongst other things. Moro was not a man prone to laughter, but he found himself having to repress a snort whenever the director read out an article he considered particularly profound, such as those entitled, for example, 'The tamandin and the death throes of humanism' or 'Being and (dis)appearances: Oscar and the new global spectacle'. In actual fact, Doctor Guido Anselmo Moro found it disturbing whenever somebody dared to observe the phenomenon from a broader vantage point than his own, and without seeking his opinion.

He, himself, was in no doubt as to what was attracting people to the Great Aviary. He regularly published reports on the anteater's health, completely fictitious reports which he embellished with an oedema, the discoloration of a pupil, or some blood-tainted mucous. Experts never failed to divine from them the symptoms of some new affliction, a malady that risked carrying off the creature within the week. And every such announcement confirmed the onset of the inevitable – with every statement, entry numbers would again increase, and crowds would flock to the aviary as once upon a time, Moro reflected, they would have flocked to the guillotine or the gallows.

But the doctor was mistaken, not everybody expected the same thing. On days when there was a big football game, it was the *calcio* fans who would be on the lookout for appearances by the tamandin: if he showed the tip of his snout, Roma was a shoe-in to win – in the internationals, his predictions counted for the whole of Italy. It was the little superstitious habit Giovanna had instigated in order to make Oscar a jewel in the local cultural crown. It's not at all clear any intervention on her part was even necessary. Numerous cults had emerged, all venerating this mute prophet, and without any assistance from her. People quoted cases of miracle healings. Of renewed fertility, of a loved one's return. The Church condemned the fact that the animal was the object of such idolatry, but in vain.

At closing time, the internal perimeter of the aviary would be covered in little folded notes which people would slip through the wire mesh of the netting.

Had Moro not been so absorbed with his telephone and his own convictions, the ethologist might perhaps have suggested that the question was not so much one of knowing why people were coming to see the tamandin, but rather *how* they were observing it. Even the zoo's cameras were unable to capture that. The cameras monitoring the spectators, outside the aviary, were attached to the top of the dome. They were able to provide estimates of crowd numbers, analyse crowd flow or record any disturbances: which only goes to show how pointless they were. In an effort to capture the world from above, one ends up seeing nothing at all.

In order to truly understand the visitors' behaviour, you would have had to lie low in the aviary, behind the reeds, for hour upon hour. Arm yourself with a pair of binoculars, and infinite patience. Ignore hunger pangs, the bladder's needs and the mosquito attacks. Or, an easier option, spend one's days in the old keeper's buried bunker. Then you might have been able to do as Salvatore did, and observe the bodies pressing forwards, all of those people constantly collecting at the wire mesh, slowly making their way around – you might have been able to catch a glimpse of the faces, the numerous shapes and sizes, decipher the movements, study this snapshot of humanity that only Salvatore was truly in a position to observe, while he drank his coffee.

And you might have reached the same conclusion he did: while the visitors scanned the bushes, while their eyes peered through the foliage, their hands were doing something quite different. It was almost imperceptible, but ever since Salvatore had first noticed it, he now saw nothing else. In the expectant silence, people were caressing each other. Couples held each other tightly. Hands were clasped, arms wrapped around waists. Heads rested gently on a shoulder, lips were placed on foreheads, hair entwined. They would grab a scrap of clothing, look for something to hold, to squeeze tightly. People wrapped their own arms around themselves, crossing their arms so they could stroke their shoulders. Hands would slide into pockets, thumbs gently rubbing the fabric, looking for skin – and sometimes even strangers would touch each other, without looking at each other, without seeking any permission. They would first brush past and then sometimes they would head off together, rendered one by the buttons of a shirt caught in the straps of a bag, or by fingers unwittingly interlaced.

And from arrow slit to arrow slit, Salvatore would follow these people with his gaze, as they slowly made their way around him, carried onwards by the crowd, and he would watch them disappear, melting into the faceless flood. Then he would shake his head, rouse himself as if from a dream and sit back down, picking up a half-open book or yesterday's newspaper, to bury himself in other stories.

Sometimes he would provide commentary on the day's top news items; speaking aloud, he would turn to the metal door which separated him from the animal, and the animal would not respond. Salvatore recognised each of its silences.

It would scratch at its shadow, it would ferret about in its bush, sometimes it would come and seek shelter under the awning, because of the heat. And then Salvatore would hear the rustling of straw, the scraping of claws on cement. He anticipated its needs just as he anticipated its moods. He would always announce his arrival, with three soft knocks on the metal door, before refilling the water trough or cleaning out its shelter – and the tamandin would allow his intrusion, with an almost invisible motion of its head or a whistling sound, and would retreat to allow the man to penetrate its territory. Between them there existed a benevolent suspicion, they were like an old married couple, each of them constantly verifying the other's presence, without ever seeking the other one out.

After closing, Salvatore would bring out his chair and set it down next to the bush. The tamandin would approach, never within arm's reach, but there it would stand, motionless. The man would then crumble a sugar lump for the little animal, and roll a bit of weed for himself. All about them, the final rays of sunshine would work their way up the tubes of the dome, pursued by the mounting darkness.

By mid-May, the areas outside the park had become the site of a veritable funfair, where souvenir vendors rubbed shoulders with gawking onlookers, tourists and the devout. Every evening, unruly camps sprang up beneath the umbrella pines of the Villa Borghese.

There was no longer any question of closing the zoo, of transforming it into some commercial shopping village or anything else for that matter. The board was trying to optimise their drawcard, and their sights were now set on the abandoned iceberg, in the garden's north-west. They could build a tamandinarium in its place, a 3D cinema or even a roller-coaster, there was no shortage of ideas. The iceberg was one of the rare vestiges from the original zoo, but nobody was envisaging Karl Hagenbeck hunched over his plans, the labourers who constructed the metallic framework, the sculptor who had transformed that mass of cement into a proud fragment of the Antarctic. Already, all the developers could see was a hillock of rubble, waiting to be cleared away. The municipality ordered a planning assessment to be carried out – which is why Giovanna now found herself in the former sea lions' pool, and why she was watching on, amused, as the experts tried to clamber to the iceberg's upper plateau.

She had not told them there was a back way which cut through the structure, she preferred to let them work it out for themselves, and admire them scaling this shabby edifice, entangled in their surveying equipment, like pseudo-mountaineers. One winter's afternoon, notwithstanding her high heels, she too had made her way over the obstacle with considerably greater ease. But some memories serve no purpose. Dead leaves crackled underfoot like antique parchment, dust rose slowly, caught in the light. With every step she took, a multitude of little grey spiders skittered ahead of her, making her nauseous at the sight of their swarming. The experts had hauled themselves up onto the promontory, she could no longer see them and she was just hoping to get back to her office when she heard shouts. *Un orso! C'è un orso!* cried the men, and one of them headed towards the edge of the plateau: he was keen to show her Rome Zoo's last polar bear, which was dangling at the end of his arm.

She circled the iceberg to meet up with them, and they stopped smiling when they saw her approaching. She snatched up the little soft toy, and cast a sweeping look around, then asked them curtly where they'd found it, how, where exactly. One of the men responded with a shrug of his shoulders, and took back the toy. It was right there, the fellow said, just like that... and he gently put the bear down next to a rock crevice, beneath an overhang but perfectly visible, like a gift set down on a table.

A few hours later, Giovanna was back in Moro's laboratory. The doctor had asked her to meet him there, and it was with some reluctance that the woman had pushed open the door to the building she had sworn never to set foot in again. They had taken out all the equipment, the test tubes, the glass beakers and the lions' cadavers – now one entire wall of the room was carpeted with screens, and the place looked like a master of the universe's control den, straight out of a spy film. The crowds of visitors were swarming across the wall, filmed from various different angles. One column of screens was dedicated to the discussion threads whose messages rolled on, silently and relentlessly. Giovanna had thought the place was deserted, before she noticed the doctor's cranium, barely poking out above the back of the leather chair.

'We could open a research centre here. Establish a new discipline. An ethology of networks ... it's a good title, don't you think?'

Giovanna wondered if he had called her in solely to flaunt his scientific knowledge or to show off his new wall of screens. Looking closely at his unadorned skull, she told herself that the little doctor must also feel very alone. A man alienated by his unbearable pride, but also by the infuriating head start he had over everybody else.

'You had it all planned out, didn't you? From the start?' she asked.

'Not all of it, no,' replied Moro. 'To be honest, I didn't think you'd be capable of creating all this … buzz. That's the right word for it, I believe?' asked the doctor, finally turning around in his chair. 'No, this I was not expecting. The last tamandin is no great shakes, it's not much more than a phantom. The rest of it? That's your creation.'

'All I've done is sell your idea,' said Giovanna, curling her lip in disgust, looking at the screens teeming with movement, a faceless multitude.

'Don't pull that face. You've saved the zoo. You know they were planning to close it? Your friend, the architect —'

'I'm no longer in touch with him,' Giovanna cut him off.

'That doesn't surprise me. An unusual specimen, if I may be permitted. A man walking along the edge of a chasm … You did notice the way he walked, didn't you?'

Giovanna turned away, losing herself in the flood of human ants crawling across the wall, and Moro was amused to see that, even as she was hiding one ear from him, the other was offered up to him as if all the better to hear him. Then he observed the way Giovanna had wrapped her arms around her body, arms that were protecting her belly, her back slightly rounded, as if to withstand a blow. And he decided he'd rather change the subject.

'I had hoped to see our dear director. You don't know where he is, do you?' he asked, and had the pleasure of seeing Giovanna's body suddenly relax; the woman released her tension with a laugh, as she listed every restaurant in the neighbourhood. She added that she, too, was absolutely starving – and after a moment's hesitation, suggested that if he hadn't eaten then perhaps they could have lunch together.

Moro answered with a smile, a smile that was neither ironic, nor condescending, and the face that lit up, behind the small spectacles, was not the face of a master of the universe. No, thought Giovanna: it was an amicable smile, a little shaky even. I fear I won't be granted the time, the doctor sighed as he stood up. See, he said, pointing at a monitor. Giovanna saw two police officers making their way down the path to the laboratory. The doctor took Giovanna's hand, and his handshake was warm and strangely firm, even formal. Then knocks rang out at the door.

Doctor Moro had not, as it happened, anticipated everything, and sometimes a single hair can be enough to foil the best-conceived plans. The man had nonetheless done what he could to leave no trace of himself from the moment he touched down at Gatwick airport, paying cash for the train that had taken him to Victoria, and for the Tube that had propelled him on to Regent's Park. He had bought a royal blue woollen overcoat, a matching umbrella and a grey hat, and eyeing his fellow passengers, he thought he looked far more the native Londoner than they did. He could even pass for a Mr Marrow, umbrella salesman, he'd thought to himself, checking for said umbrella at his side, and also, more importantly, for the little flask hidden in his pocket. He had saluted the big portrait painted on the wall of the station at Baker Street, and had set off on foot across Regent's Park. But it was an utterly unexpected sunny day for November, and the umbrella salesman had started sweating heavily, irritated to note that Regent's Park was not the Villa Borghese. After kilometres of flowering garden beds and beautifully manicured lawns, his jealousy had erupted upon seeing the line of people anxiously queuing for the ticket booths at the London Zoo. When it came his turn, he had curtly declined to buy a paperback guide, or make a gift to the baboons, or receive the newsletter of the ZSL, and had ended up walking away from the ticket office completely exasperated. The attendant had had to run after him to hand him his change and his umbrella, both of which he had left behind on the counter.

Which is why she remembered him, that particular fellow. Ah, yes, she was quite certain it was the man on the video: umbrella, thick blue coat and a grey hat, in that heat – the poor man's face was covered in sweat and he had this peculiar way of speaking, hand in front of his mouth, like this, two fingers held over his moustache, as if it might fall off. The security manager thanked the ticket-seller – behind his back, Nadia Monk let out a *fucking told you*, and a sigh of relief. After considering the tamandin hairs and the merino wool fibres, the investigators then turned their attention to the hairs of the fake moustache, and to the man who was wearing it. They were easily able to trace his path through the zoo, see him arrive at the tamandins' enclosure, and see how he wiped his moist hand on his woollen coat before then tipping out the contents of his flask. How, with a generous gesture, he scattered twenty or so *Amblyomma improbum* ticks, their veins gorged with virus. How he did the same at the armadillos and at the okapis, to cover his tracks, and how he made it back to Euston station just in time for the 11.40 am train to Chester.

That afternoon, while Doctor Guido Anselmo Moro was attending an international conference on ungulate reproduction, with neither remorse nor pseudonym, the ticks had started the work that ticks do. Perched on a stalk of grass, they had set about waiting for a bit of animal warmth to wander past: it was all in the natural order of things, or almost.

That year, the little anteater haunted the window displays of the purveyors of culture. Writers and film directors had latched on to the topic from the first murmurs of public interest, and well before Moro's arrest: films were shot, edited, distributed and forgotten in the space of a few months, novels were sold, the ink having had no time to dry, their pages, thus, illegible. It was typical of an era where facts and their representation overlapped. At the start of this new century, humans were no longer building anything of any significance, they were content simply to react: in this, they were behaving a little more like other animals.

The only fiction which left a lasting impression on the public was a cartoon, a Franco-Belgian coproduction called *Tam the Tamandin* – in English-speaking countries, the show was sold under the name *Anty the Anteater*. Armed with rounded claws and a big heart, Tam would jump from branch to branch to save animals in danger, caught in the snares of ill-shaven poachers. With the help of his two best friends, Daniel and Valerie, he prevented oil tankers from crashing into coastlines, protected baby seals or warned of nuclear power station explosions. Tam was such a success that he replaced the real Oscar in the eyes of the younger viewing public, and his smiling effigy was reproduced on thousands of school satchels.

Ever since finding the toy bear the previous week, Giovanna's bouts of nausea had disappeared. She had tidied up her things and cleared her desk, all under the watchful eye of the fluffy toy, and then she had gently set it down on the pile of old files and papers to be thrown away.

There were still twenty minutes before opening time, the sound of walkie-talkies crackled along the path, they were getting ready to receive the human wave that was foaming at the gates, and Giovanna made her way ahead of the breaker with tranquil step, down side alleys dappled with sunlight. A peacock crossed her path, its train sweeping the dust, and for the first time, she realised what a great burden to the bird its extraordinary plumage must be. Its entire existence was devoted to that moment of seduction, and it was doubtless the same for most creatures: they meet, they embrace, they disappear.

She made her way past the ruminating, aloof silhouette of a dromedary. This was where they had met, at precisely this spot, and now the dromedary's fleece was shedding in thick woolly rags which covered the ground. Chahine had gone. He had left behind a bear, he had acknowledged her in his own peculiar manner and that was fine, it was even quite sufficient to allow her to move on to other things. The gardens had swallowed up the foreigner, that was all, the zoo had gnawed away at him, had reduced him to fragments, to scraps of shoes, to shirt buttons. And had one searched through the remains strewn across the lions' rock, one would most likely have discovered human bones, Algerian bones, architect's bones.

She found herself next to the lake. On the wooden bridge, in the shade of the willows. The water was covered in pollen, a swan was paddling away, drawing a great black triangle in its wake. Giovanna allowed her imagination to slip across the stagnant waters. It was so much easier to write your own endings – and how she now understood those people who came seeking a little comfort, here, in the presence of the tamandin's mute silence. She took the passport from her pocket. She hesitated one last time, rifling the edges of the pages, black water below her.

Five days later, Giovanna received confirmation that Chahine had indeed not only left the zoo, but also Rome and Italian soil. As she crossed the threshold of the diplomatic mission, she too felt as though she were suddenly elsewhere – not in North Africa, nor in an Arab country or former French colony, because Giovanna had not the slightest idea what those words might encompass. There were just minor peculiarities, a customer service desk bizarrely located in the basement, the pink walls of the waiting room, dominated by a poster advertising the merits of Air Algérie and which must, judging by the flight attendant's uniform, have dated from the 1960s. A smell of detergent and files.

Chahine had gone there three weeks earlier, in order to obtain a new travel document. He had passed through this same room, he had found himself standing in front of the glass panes at that same counter, and Giovanna wondered what language he would have used to speak to the receptionist, and whether he had had any problems providing valid passport photos. Perhaps he had tried to use the same photos as at the zoo: face partially turned away, a skittering look, angled downwards. But she preferred to imagine that this time the man had stared directly into the lens, that he wasn't some wavering ghost-like presence who had crossed the room, but an individual in full possession of his faculties, a man who wanted, simply, to return home. In any event this is what she deduced from the ambassador's account, even if she would rather have found out a little less.

When the receptionist had announced that His Excellency was ready to see her, Giovanna had protested weakly – she had just come to hand in a passport that had been lost at the zoo, as discussed on the telephone. But the employee had insisted on accompanying her upstairs, and all the way through to the imposing office of her superior. A man in his sixties with salt-and-pepper hair, elegant and affable – too affable, for Giovanna's taste, and more loquacious than his role required of him. He had been delighted to receive her call, and to recover the passport; as she would be aware, the document was the property of the Algerian state, he would like to thank her formally for its return, not everybody would have taken the trouble, and so forth.

The diplomat had taken the situation quite to heart, although it was only a consular matter. The passport which Giovanna was returning in fact belonged to one of the nation's renowned architects, an architect who had 'won competitions', and who taught at the University of Algiers. Chahine Gharbi was a heritage expert, he had taken up the cause of some remnant colonial architecture which had earned him a little notoriety and a not inconsiderable number of enemies, the ambassador had explained, while pouring Giovanna a refreshment she had not requested. The fact remains that the accident had put an end to all that. A sad story indeed, yes, the ambassador continued, one which could happen to anybody, an unfortunate traffic accident that had cost his daughter her life. His career, he added, had suffered enormously.

As if in a dream, Giovanna had accepted the glass held out to her by the man, a finely cut and impossibly heavy glass, so heavy she almost dropped it. She went over to the window. Outside, pedestrians were clinging to the walls in order to escape the heat of the sun. All these destinies intersecting before our very eyes, said the ambassador, joining her. But you must be used to that, at the zoo, with all those people coming through, you would be familiar with all of these issues, all those little individual requests. We have so many nationals declared missing at the moment, you cannot imagine. We moved heaven and earth for Gharbi, apparently he had come here to work on a project, and then *pooffff,* the ambassador blew out the word, waving his hand, he disappeared, no news of him for months. His wife was calling every day, poor woman. And one morning, he just resurfaces, as if nothing had happened, wanting a new passport. Just imagine, no hint of an explanation from him, not one word. What do you do, ours is a thankless task ... it's the lot of those with significant responsibilities, you wouldn't disagree.

As he spoke, the ambassador had drawn closer to her. And as for you, what an extraordinary phenomenon, that anteater, I'm envious. What a spectacle. Might you do us the honour of dining with us, one evening? Have you ever tried a tagine? My wife would be delighted to meet you.

Giovanna smiled, making no attempt to conceal her weariness as she looked down at the glass which at no point had she lifted to her lips. She returned it to the ambassador without a word, and acknowledged him with a nod of her head, but the man insisted: did she think it might be possible to organise a private visit? For members of the diplomatic corps? His eyes were shining now, and Giovanna took a step backwards, murmuring another acknowledgement before she reached the door, wait, the ambassador flung the words after her, it would be such an honour for us, to see Oscar up close, he cried, pursuing Giovanna out to the stairs. She turned around and, sighing, told him the zoo did not organise private visits. That in any event she was unable to assist him, she no longer worked there.

She rushed down the last steps and past the security guards, head down, like a thief.

The Passion of the tamandin played out in July. It was warm, that evening, and all Rome was sleeping with their windows open. Everybody heard the shot. The campers squatting around the Villa Borghese. The stallholders sleeping in their makeshift huts. The *carabinieri* on their beat, around the zoo's perimeters, and the security guards patrolling within the grounds. The gunshot ripped through the night, but the noise was followed by a silence so profound that people doubted having heard a thing, and gave up looking for the cause.

It was only the next day, on the rounds carried out prior to the zoo's opening, that the body was discovered. The impact had thrown it far from its bush, towards the pond – a small shapeless mass, flies buzzing around it. The keeper was found in the adjacent shelter, prostrate over his stool, hands clasped together, eyes vacant. Lying at his feet, a shotgun.

News spread like wildfire, a spark that leaped from security guard to keeper, from keeper to ticket-seller, from ticket-seller to waiter, all the way to the visitors gathered at the gates, sending shockwaves through the crowd – Leonardi had to be evacuated as a matter of urgency: his colleagues led the stupefied keeper to the administration building, its windows already shattering as they were struck by stones, while a police car fought its way down Via dei Parioli, so the suspect could be loaded up and taken as far away as possible, foot to the floor, sirens off, to some police station on the city's outskirts. The crowd was already running towards the police station closest to the zoo, metal bars in hand, their eyes burning with rage.

All of this took place before any news outlet was able to relay the death, by shooting, of Oscar the anteater. The first images to be circulated on the networks were those of a civil war unfolding in Rome's northern suburbs, cars ablaze, an upended tram, clashes which took authorities an entire day to settle. One after the other, their various spokespeople promised that the zookeeper, Salvatore Leonardi, would have to face the full force of the law, and that he would, quite lawfully, be lynched.

At long last, the journalists were able to bring out Oscar's obituaries which had been languishing in their drawers. On Twitter, stars and artists hastened to bid farewell to the last specimen of *Tamandinus tubulidentatus*, minutes of silence were organised online. An editorial in *Le Monde* compared the extinction of an animal species to the disappearance of a star from the firmament – it was a beautiful image and, if one thought about it, the two events carried exactly the same significance. A portrait of the assassin, Leonardi, was painted, against the backdrop of the tragedy. The public's curiosity was endless, but there was barely enough material to satisfy it – it needed embellishing, expanding and spinning out, there just wasn't much to say about the old bachelor who was both chatty and uncomplicated, was discreet in his personal relations, and a conscientious zookeeper, like his father. Declarations of disbelief followed from neighbours, childhood friends. Leonardi had no reason to be unhappy, his colleagues were adamant, especially as he'd been about to retire.

In the absence of a discernible motive, the court of public opinion decided the man was evil incarnate. And the face of evil incarnate filled many pages of magazines, including the one which Giovanna was leafing through several days after the event. A magazine left lying around in a gynaecologist's waiting room, which she had idly flicked through: the single available photo of him had been so photoshopped she had not at first recognised Salvatore Leonardi's face, his wrinkles were deeper, his eyebrows and pupils darker. She struggled to remember what the keeper really looked like, and was as moved by the tamandin's death as by any one of the thousand tragedies that make up the news every day – she was otherwise preoccupied at the moment, and would simply have preferred the world to be a little more stable, a little less violent. When it came her turn, she abandoned the magazine to the draughty waiting room, to ennui and indifference.

It was a carefully guarded secret, a secret which did not feature in any magazine. A few lines which ought to have been included in the autopsy report, and which remained unwritten. There were three of them that morning – the director, the new veterinarian and a biologist from La Sapienza, still wearing his pyjama top – all there to examine the tamandin's corpse which they had carried through to the medical annex, while outside continued the people's frenzied calls for prosecution and punishment.

The tamandin appeared strangely thin now, lying there stretched out. The tip of its long snout was dry, its eyes closed. Its body appeared intact, apart from a few slightly raised scales, halfway up its spine. The vet postulated that the animal had sensed danger, that it had stood up on its hind paws, lifting its claws and presenting its thorax to the shooter – the shot must have been a direct hit to its heart. White gloves gently rolled the creature over onto its back, revealing the wound. Hairs were glued together around a still glistening, gaping hole, out of which marched a cohort of ants, interrupted in their vengeful task. The doctor plunged in his tweezers, and had no difficulty at all extracting the bullet which had, he said, slammed into the third dorsal vertebra – a small metallic mass which he held up to the light, its provenance and calibre to be confirmed by a ballistic examination, seven millimetres, the vet estimated, perhaps eight, but he stopped talking when he saw that everybody had stopped listening. Dumbfounded, the director was staring where the biologist was pointing with a trembling finger. When the cadaver had been turned onto its back, the rear paws had gently spread apart.

The biologist started stammering something about the retracted organs of myrmecophages, and the veterinarian started searching for said organs with a quivering finger, organs which were not there. The three men were sweating heavily now, their eyes riveted to the unbearable absence. They beat a cautious retreat to the back of the room, speaking in strangled murmurs, every now and again throwing glances at the creature, as if it might have been able to hear them. Nobody, in all these years, had bothered to verify the received wisdom. They could have blamed Moro, seeing as he, in any event, was a lost cause, but the institution would never recover from such a blow. And the hunched men kept glancing at the animal out of the corner of their eyes, as if now seeing a demon. In unveiling its sex, the creature had affirmed one miniscule part of its identity, a truth which eluded all that had been said, written or thought about it.

Not another word was uttered by the men that morning, and their silence hung heavy as an oath. The incinerator was turned on, the thing slipped in. A state funeral was hastily organised.

The following week, the tamandin's ashes were scattered over the lake, under the watchful gaze of the crowd gathered on the banks. There was a little orchestra. Some people prayed for Oscar's soul, remembering that he had been blessed at the celebration of Saint Anthony the Abbot. For two weeks, the gates of the zoo were strewn with flowers.

A few months later, in January 2011, the Rome Zoo was exactly one hundred years old. In the ordinary course, humans accord a certain significance to figures, especially if they contain zeros – this time, they considered it more prudent to ignore the anniversary. We would have liked to describe a magnificent day of gates flung open, a spectacular butterfly release, to celebrate together the endurance of this grand idea, and to listen to the mayor of Rome recap, in a poignant speech, how animals and humans had lived side by side, in the city, for this past century. But it was unclear what lessons to draw from a history people were more interested in forgetting. The institution was emerging from the storm Oscar had unleashed, weakened and wavering. A fortune was spent reopening paths, re-doing enclosures; two giraffes, an elephant and a large snake were bought on the quiet, a new lion was welcomed. And in order to ensure its reputation was forgotten, the institution, once again, changed its name.

The zoo is now called the Bioparco di Roma. Its attendance levels are the same as those of other European zoos, it is bustling on the weekend and the rest of the time it is empty. Every now and again, themed exhibits are displayed which are, to a greater or lesser degree, timely: in 2015, when the media's attention is focused on the thousands of migrants seeking to cross the Mediterranean, the Bioparco stages an exhibition called *Alien Fish – the invasion of our waters*. Festooned with ferocious exotic fish, the exhibition's posters go up alongside those of xenophobic political parties in the city's streets. And if the Rome Zoo is no longer making history, it continues to serve as its bitter reflection.

Its visitors today are very different from those who attended its opening. In the space of a century, humans have had time to change ideologies, haircuts and dress styles, repeatedly. But the lion watching them wander past, from its position at the back of its enclosure, has remained exactly the same. Its mane is gleaming just as it did two thousand years ago, when it would make its way across the sand of the Colosseum, and its husky roar, its growl that came from the depths of time, still raises hairs on human necks. And so, visitors still have a tendency to gauge, with a glance, the width of the moats, the diameter of the bars, the thickness of the glass viewing panes – all the precautions which separate them from the beasts, while still allowing them to enjoy the spectacle. For they remain entranced by that grace, by that strength which reminds them of the fragility of their own body, their ageing hunter-gatherer bodies which somehow they are no longer quite sure how to use, and which they struggle to maintain in good working condition. They envy the constancy of those proud animals, which reduces their own grander ambitions to mere hiccups.

And while species might well have become extinct, with animals dying in their thousands, they continue to evade human domination. They are perfectly free to roam through the history of their cities, as they have no need to follow any particular direction, nor to provide any meaning. What endures, both in them and through them, is all that remains unwritten – everything beyond the reach of historians, everything rumbling away beneath the surface of written accounts, everything that is teeming in their shadows.

The first round of keepers had already passed through when Chahine ventured towards the water's edge. He went there every night, would sit on the same bench, imagining the murmuring of the big fountain in the middle of the lake. Powerful jets of water, jets describing majestic arcs, their spray cooling the visitors to his shopping precinct. He scratched his beard, he was still wavering as to the precise form it should take. Sometimes a man would sit down next to him. He would set his hat down on the bench and nod earnestly in agreement. Architects understand one another, even separated by three generations: De Vico agreed with Chahine, the lake was missing something. He, himself, envisaged an island, an island or a system of little islets, linked by Japanese bridges. Make no mistake, I know my fountains, de Vico insisted, but here, beneath the trees, it's not a fountain you need. Chahine would then scratch his head vigorously, de Vico had this blinkered bucolic approach to urban landscaping, he was obsessed by the decorative, when instead spaces should be pared back. The Italian answered him with a lopsided smile, a smile that was both patient and knowing. Sure, the Algerian then admitted, your aviary isn't bad. But I'm going to tear it down, too, in fact that's the first thing I'm going to do, Chahine announced, standing up. De Vico paled, so pale he became transparent. I'm joking, said Chahine, and de Vico's colour started slowly to return, before he disappeared altogether.

Then Chahine undid his tie, grabbed his briefcase and walked off. These work meetings often meant he would arrive late to school, and Nour, who would be the last one left at the front gate, would greet him with shining eyes, and a smile so bright he would feel guiltier still. It was on one of those evenings, in the car, that he had promised to take her to the zoo. And then he had kept putting his promise off, from one Friday to the next – but Nour had forgiven him, since, here she was anyway, running from one enclosure to another, laughing, slipping through cages to pat the tigers, she really was fearless, thought her father, following her. Only the bisons really intimidated her, when they spilled out onto the path and blocked their way. Then the little girl would run back to hold his hand, he would bend over slightly, and their two silhouettes would watch the panting procession, the rumbling hooves and steaming fleece, she holding her breath, he silently enjoying the small hand slipped into his own.

And then she, too, would disappear, and Chahine would be left holding nothing but a white plastic bag, a plastic bag with a soft bear, which he had bought her. And the pointless bag would swing against his leg, and its rustling would give rhythm to the darkness. From far off in the distance came the dull beat of a party. The scent of the crowds still hung over the paths, the sweat of thousands of people. As for his own odour, Chahine was no longer aware of it, only every now and again would he catch a sour waft – and he would wash himself in the bathrooms, ancient bathrooms whose lock he had forced, and whose taps spat out a brownish stream. He took the chance to shave and to gather his thoughts, he tried to hold his gaze, in the mirror. Of course, he had to leave this place. But despite consulting the map of the zoo, spreading it out over the cold tiles, smoothing out its creases, running his fingers over it with their blackened nails, he could no longer read it. The lines were blurry, every building which had ever been built was superimposed one on top of the other, along with every animal that had ever lived there, it was nothing more than a series of scribbles, and again Chahine picked up a pen to try to decipher his way through, a way out, and the tip of his pen would end up losing itself in the intersections of lines and worn-out folds of paper.

The simplest thing would have been to call reception, to get some instructions, he rummaged through his pockets and remembered he had lost his telephone a long time ago, or had thrown it into the lake, one evening, and he remembered, too, that he was now living in an iceberg, where there was no reception desk, nor keys to ask for, which offered considerable advantages, in terms of privacy. And once again Chahine remembered that he wasn't mad, contrary to appearances, but that it would all the same be preferable to talk to somebody about that, to get a second opinion.

Then he would plunge back into the darkness. The street lamps were out now, and the air was rich with the smells of sap, of earth and manure. The rustling of animals blended with the sound of his own steps. The cry of a tawny owl, distant yowling. From time to time, a torch light swept the paths, but you could see it coming from a long way off – Chahine would then slip into the shadowy undergrowth or behind a hut, and Nour, next to him, would burst into laughter. Her father would place a finger in front of her mouth, making big round eyes, which made the little girl laugh even harder, and Chahine would chortle too, and he could see at his feet the blade of light searching through the grass, searching the undergrowth, lingering before sweeping away once more. He was not afraid, he knew all the blind spots – he could wend his way through the park from shadow to shadow, until the end of time.

Many are the tourists who stroll around the Janiculum Hill to admire all of Rome stretching out before them, the sea of bells and cupolas that catch fire in the setting sun. They are oblivious to the fact that halfway along the path, between the Manfredi Lighthouse and Piazza Garibaldi, the promenade overlooks an old convent that has, since the 19th century, housed the Regina Cœli prison. And to the fact that the prison is now home to the murderer, Salvatore Leonardi. Tourists who linger on the terrace promenade are thus sometimes surprised to see passers-by leaning over the edge, cupping their hands to project their voice and yelling out a few curses, a few local, well-chosen insults, in the hope they will reach their target, the monster's cell.

But the prison's board had put their inmate in the far wing, together with the paedophiles and wife-killers, in the protection of solitary confinement. His file noted an eight-year sentence, with a minimum four years non-parole, for 'animal cruelty'. It was the only distinguishing feature in an otherwise unremarkable file: no religion, no dietary requirements. His record had been quickly filled out, as quickly as his pockets had been emptied when he was arrested: a heavy bunch of keys, a red cigarette lighter and some tobacco. And in his back pocket a sheet of paper, folded in four, which would have cast some light on the keeper's actions, had anybody bothered to read it.

Salvatore Leonardi belonged to a generation for whom the printed word carried a certain weight, all the more so if the words appeared on a piece of paper with letterhead, signature and stamp. He was unaware that a document was able to be generated automatically by some computer system, nonchalantly spat out by a printer, distractedly signed, thoughtlessly enclosed in an envelope, and prematurely left in his pigeonhole, along with his pay slips, meal vouchers and the usual monthly paperwork. The letter contained an obscure calculation of points, a table scattered with tax-related acronyms, sums to be received and deducted pursuant to the new framework now applicable to S. Leonardi, a former Category 8, subclass B employee, who at the end of this month will have completed his period of active employment.

Folding the letter back up, Salvatore Leonardi did not imagine there to be any recourse. He simply figured his time was up, and that he was done with being afraid. As night fell, he had given one last sugar lump to the animal, and that evening the anteater's snooping snout had almost come looking for it right out of the palm of his hand. Then Salvatore had taken out the old shotgun. The butt nestled perfectly into the curve of his shoulder, just as it had nestled perfectly into his father's shoulder and his grandfather's shoulder, just as it would never again nestle into any other shoulder, as Leonardi had no children, and nobody to whom he could tell this story.

Had he had a son, he would have described to him the burden of his duty, and the nature of the ties that bind man to beast. He would have told him how, to prop up his courage, he had imagined the tamandin at the mercy of some colleague who would have shown it off, at the end of a leash, to wealthy visitors of an evening. Or who would have removed one of its claws, to satisfy some collector. Had Salvatore had a son, perhaps he would have admitted to him how his finger had trembled, on the trigger, and how at the last moment the old animal had been frightened, because he, Salvatore Leonardi, was made of different stuff to his forebears. But in any case, the keeper had neither son nor wife to tell.

And so he had remained silent, before the judge, as he had done before the lawyer. And he had remained silent, too, in the company of the prison guards who, mocking and conspiratorial, had plied him with questions about the hours he had spent with the animal, about his work as a keeper. You and me, we see eye to eye, they persevered, offering him cigarettes, and later Salvatore learned that journalists were pacing backwards and forwards outside the prison gates, and that they were ready to pay out for the slightest confidence. The chaplain was the only person from whom he accepted visits, because he came to find him much later on, and then almost every week. The man had started by recounting the lives of Saint Francis of Assisi and of Saint Anthony of Padua, and then the story of Jonah who had been saved by the whale, of Elijah being fed by the ravens, and of the dog who accompanied the good Tobias. And sometimes Salvatore would correct the chaplain, because he knew the stories better than he did. But he never agreed to a confession. One day, the man announced that he had been allocated to some other position, and that he would no longer be coming. But he had something for Salvatore: he had opened his palm and handed him a snail, which he had found in the prison yard.

The snail had chosen to reside in a corner of the cell, near the ceiling. In the days' waning light, Salvatore could see the gleaming lines traced by the mollusc, meanderings which suddenly were illuminated, revealing a drawing only he could see. Then the shadows would climb, the grilles and locks would slam one last time, slowly the walls around Salvatore would start to dissolve, and he would lose himself in the pathways of his memories.

One night in May, as he sat under the aviary's dome, the keeper had heard steps. A wan-looking figure had emerged from the darkness, had placed his hands on the wire netting and had stared at him silently. Salvatore took him for a prowler, given his beard and rags. The man had pulled a piece of paper from his pocket, he wanted something. So the keeper had suggested he walk around the structure, and had gone out to meet him. He had recognised the stranger, despite his long hair, his burning gaze and torn clothing.

Salvatore had always appreciated this patient and attentive visitor. They didn't speak the same language, but a smile was all that was needed to sweep away any awkwardness, a smile and a shrug of the shoulders: the meaning of the words was not so important, they made themselves understood. That night, the stranger had greeted him as if they had seen each other just the night before, he had shown him the map he was holding, like a tourist who had lost his way. A crumpled brochure, blackened, ragged. Salvatore had brought him into the shelter, had reheated some soup which the man had hurriedly gulped down, burning hot. He had returned often.

The keeper would bring two chairs out from the shelter, which he would set down in the middle of the aviary, under the black beech, next to the little pond. It didn't take much for it to feel comfortable, it only needed the stranger, for example, to take out the chairs himself. Or that he surprise Salvatore by bringing some food which he must have filched from the refreshment stall. They would settle in, flip the lid off a bottle. Bats would dance in the halo glow of the lamplight, outside the shelter. Sometimes a satellite would shine, in the firmament, which they might point a finger at and watch as it passed over, slowly, through the mesh of the aviary. And the keeper would forget he was dealing with a madman, or with somebody who was, let us say, madder than he himself was, relatively speaking. They could even laugh about it, when the stranger suddenly tapped his index finger against his temple, with a chuckle. His delirium would arrive in waves. He could take the keeper for somebody else, talk to him in French, point at the aviary and go to stroke the structure and return to congratulate him, with raised thumb and a pat on the shoulder, as if Salvatore had designed it himself. Then the man would sit back down, scratch his head, his madness retreating. Together they would listen to the murmurings of the animal-filled night, to the silence of the stars.

The anteater had also accepted the stranger. The creature would come and ferret about next to his chair, right up against the gaping soles of his shoes. That night, Salvatore had indicated to the tamandin with his chin, and then, in the air, he had drawn the curvy outlines of a female silhouette. The stranger had smiled, although he had probably not understood the significance of the confidence just shared. Perhaps he did not even know that thousands of visitors crowded the paths, by day, and that they were all coming to see that animal there, which they, wrongheadedly, called Oscar. None of this appeared to bother him.

That night Salvatore had repeated his gesture, the outline of a woman, pointing at the stranger. The man had nodded his head: yes, he used to have one. But his hand told the story of her being far away. The wind had picked up, making the leaves of the black beech rustle, the tamandin swept the earth with its tail, backwards and forwards between the two men, its trunk-like snout raised. Than Salvatore asked another question, one hand held at a child's height. And again Chahine nodded, he described a girl with long hair, and his fingers indicated the number seven. But now, his joined palms explained, the little girl was sleeping. Salvatore frowned. The stranger's hands trembled, on his knees. They rose up again, together, hesitant. And then they took hold of an invisible steering wheel, a steering wheel which the man gripped hard – and in his trembling hands the steering wheel turned sharply right, then hard left and Salvatore heard the brakes squeal and the deafening noise of crumpling metal. Then a great silence. The stranger was gasping. Salvatore placed a hand on his shoulder and the man turned towards him. His face had disappeared, his features undone by the darkness.

They had left the aviary, a few hours before dawn. They had walked a long time, side by side, not looking at each other. The stranger had gathered his things from the iceberg, and then Salvatore had led him to the main gate. The man had shaken his hand, and his silhouette had slipped away into the night.

Following the 2013 municipal elections, Giovanna had returned to the town council. The new mayor had grand plans, she had reconnected with her former colleagues, there was a good feeling in the air. But as each day drew to a close, Giovanna would keep her eyes glued to the clock above her desk.

It had taken exactly three million years and nine months for her son to be brought into the world: surely that warranted her going home a little earlier, in the evenings. Her husband thought so, he was besotted with this pint-sized little person who bore his name, and who looked so much like Giovanna. Every evening was a celebration, and despite their weariness the couple were never done with their hushed marvelling at this child they were no longer waiting for.

Their apartment was filled with bright colours and animals in their hundreds. It had started with countless soft toys, piled up under the blankets. And then animals had appeared on the walls of the little bedroom, they had covered the refrigerator door, slipped into the bookshelves, haunting the pages of every big illustrated book. The wildest of the creatures were heaped up in a cane basket: monstrous beetles mixed with miniscule zebras and elephants in every size, fluorescent chameleons, cheetahs with twisted paws, soft crabs and giraffe-yellow tigers. And every day the basket would be tipped up, and the animals would head off to colonise the apartment, from the hall through to the bathroom. Entire herds would be found under the furniture, a dusty, colourful muddle – accompanied, every now and again, by a real spider which the mother would hurriedly dispatch, in front of the wide-eyed child.

Giovanna had never returned to the zoo. Or perhaps just once or twice, for a quiet, solitary afternoon. Shadows whispered in the magnolias, light shone through the maple leaves, rendered paper-thin by the autumn. In three years the place had hardly changed, she lost her way every time.

With thanks to Serena, Louis and Anouk, for opening the doors to the zoo, each in their own way. To Nancy and Guy, for their support. And also to Delphine Reist, Sofiane Hadj-adj, Nicolas Couchepin, Adriano and Ruth Theus Baldassarre for their illuminating comments and insights.

I could not have written this novel without the help of Spartaco Gippoliti (*La Giungla di Villa Borghese*, Belvedere) and Mauro Picone (*Uomini dentro le gabbie*, Testudo). I thank them for their invaluable information and for so generously making themselves available.

Philippe Rahmy was there to witness the genesis of this work, and I felt his heartening presence accompanying me through to its final lines. This book is dedicated to him.